UNEXPECTED MEDITATIONS

UNEXPECTED MEDITATIONS
LATE IN THE TWENTIETH CENTURY

by
James V. Schall

FRANCISCAN HERALD PRESS

Unexpected Meditations Late in the Twentieth Century by James V. Schall. Copyright © 1985 by Franciscan Herald Press, 1434 West 51st Street, Chicago, Illinois 60609. All rights reserved.

Library of Congress Cataloging in Publication Data

Schall, James V.
    Unexpected meditations late in the twentieth century.

    1. Meditations. 2. Schall, James V. I. Title.
BX2182.2.S34   1985   242   85-10126
ISBN 0-8199-0885-1

The time of human life is but a point, and the substance is a flux, and its perceptions dull, and the composition of the body corruptible, and the soul a whirl, and fortune inscrutable, and fame a senseless thing. In a word, everything which belongs to the body is a flowing stream, and what belongs to the soul a dream and a vapor, and life is a warfare and a stranger's sojourn, and future fame is oblivion. What then is there which can guide a man? One thing and only one, philosophy.

–*Marcus Aurelius, Meditations, II, 17.*

You have been obedient to the truth and purified your souls until you can love like brothers, in sincerity; let your love for each other be real and from the heart—your new birth was not from any mortal seed but from the everlasting word of the living and eternal God. "All flesh is grass and its glory like the wild flower's. The grass withers, the flower falls, but the word of the Lord remains forever." What is this word? It is the Good News that has been brought to you.

—*I Peter, 1:22-25.*

TABLE OF CONTENTS

Introduction

About these reflections, little enough need be said. Yet there are certain initial remarks that are needed to clarify my comings and goings over the years, for there will be in these pages much, not necessarily in an orderly sequence of time, about places where I have been for a while. What can be noted too, in the beginning, is that this is a way, my way undoubtedly, of looking at our often chaotic lives and loves and foibles, all of which are intertwined. But this too is a "way" which I conceive to be a "spiritual" exercise, if I can use that exalted term for a very pedestrian sort of journey. We need a consciousness, as we go along, about the manner in which lived events begin to fall together or, perhaps more often, fall apart. In this sense, then, I remain a teacher of whose who would see.

Too, this is written by someone peculiar enough to think that the most sensible context in which to illumine what we do, of what happens to us in our personal world, is, while neglecting neither philosophy nor science nor the poets, a religious one. I do not think this from some sort of lofty abstraction or doctrine, however. The other alternatives are there to be tried and investigated. I have taken a look at most of them myself. But there is much they do not explain. Even the philosophy in which Marcus Aurelius, the Emperor, put so much hope, after he had despaired of all else, seems not enough, even for philosophers, even for Emperors.

This is a minority opinion, I suppose. But available alternatives have always left me weary and empty. Nonetheless, this is not intended to be apologetic, even if it remains something of an "apology" in the sense in which a

Plato or a Newman used the word, an account of a life. This book is merely what it says it is — *Meditations* late in our century. They are also "*Unexpected* Meditations" because I think life is like that, quite unexpected, beginning from the fact that we begin. However much we hear talk of planning births of our kind, we all seem somehow unexpected and unplanned when we actually show up looking out on this world, wondering what it is all about.

A model for this way of looking at what exists can be found, however. I have long been struck, as I shall explain, by the *Meditations* of the Roman Emperor, Marcus Aurelius. His Stoic way of viewing the world is surely one of the powerful testimonies we have about our fate. Indeed, almost two thousand years after his time, it is still most difficult to see why his view of the world was not correct. And this is what these *meditations* are—Christian broodings about the questions an ancient man asked himself, about the difference the two millennia have made in the way a human life sees itself.

Marcus Aurelius stands there, quiet on his frontier or in his study, ready to receive back those who no longer believe. We think there are many other places besides his to which we might go, but none seems so attractive, or perhaps so logical, as that of the Roman Emperor. And yet, if we go his way, it is because we have chosen a lesser vision, though a vision still, and a defensible one. So I will arrange my thoughts here as he did, in twelve books or chapters, with individual, numbered notes, all somehow flowing from what he remarked. However, these are my remarks, not forgetting that men such as the Roman Emperor are in our backgrounds, certainly in my background.

Meditations, of course, can be read slowly or quickly. They do not have to be read in sequence, though there is a kind of personal progression that is evident in all we do because human life is concrete and particular. We are there to watch it. We can account, after a time, for names, places, conversations, more than for abstract theories and ideas, which the philosophers tell us are somehow "eternal," that is, they are always the same when a mind thinks them. Much of what is "unique" about my own life is here. Places, persons, readings, letters, moods — these are things that have happened to me, have struck me. We cannot begin from where someone else is, a blessing of sorts. Nor should we worry about trying to do so. Aristotle, I believe, asked whether we would want complete happiness on the condition that we would be someone else. He calmly said we wouldn't. He was right.

The times and places that come up again and again in an apparently haphazard way in these meditations — Rome, San Francisco, Iowa, Washington, places in between — are not intended to confuse. This is the way most of us experience life and its meanings. We go from place to place. We suddenly realize that what we are thinking about, recalling, happened a decade ago. We can explain why we were in, say, Boston or Philadelphia or Freiburg or St. Louis on such and such a day, yet it seems strange and accidental, too, that we were actually there. There is something mysterious about it all. We are all plunged into a kind of interminable chaos. By not trying to obscure the often bewildering changes, thoughts, encounters, labors, and events that happen to us, we can find a more realistic and helpful "way" to see how, through our reflections on real actions in the world, our world, things begin to fit together.

The "times and places" recounted here are my times and places. Yet, often they are times and places familiar to most people. If where we were or what we did or thought were so radically different that no one could imagine what they were like, the great bond of human interconnection would be finally broken. For a time, from 1964, I lived in Europe, in Rome mostly, though I lived in Ghent one year and was in Germany and England often. But I also spent a semester each year at the University of San Francisco, and after 1978, I have been in Washington. I seem still to be going back and forth a good deal from one coast to another, not so much to Europe any more.

So I will appear ever to be moving on, ever moving to or between places. This travel has given me, I suppose, a constant sense of the impermanence of our homes, as well as an acute consciousness of our desire for stability. Yet, travel itself is an ancient sign, a sign of passingness, of the scriptural notion that we are but pilgrims and wayfarers, wanderers. The very symbol of a city like Rome, which indeed is still called "Eternal," is, as periodic Holy Years are intended to remind us, that here is a place we know even before going there. And on leaving it, we recall it because it is already a part of our very selves. So it is a place, like all places, from which we eventually leave, a place I too have now left, though I remember it vividly.

Sometimes, I have flown, always between continents. In spite of all the advice I had about taking a ship someday, I never did. Oftentimes, in Europe or in the States, I have taken a bus or a train or a car. Walking is still the best way to see, when you are once there. I have walked much in these pages. I do not always like to go the same route, though some places I never tire of, places and people I see as frequently as I can. This has been an odd sort of existence, to be sure. But it has been mine, and I have been content with it, at least insofar as we can be fully content with anything in this life, which is not designed, I think, for full contentment.

These are entitled, then, "Meditations." And that title is not wholly arbitrary. This is not the classical "meditation manual" of a type that used to be common several decades ago, books that are worth our effort still to peruse once in a while. However, all that happens to us — what we brood about, the people we meet, letters we happen to receive, books and stories we read, chance conversations, accidents, sicknesses, duties we may have — such are replete with spirit and life. We should be sure that they do not pass us by completely unnoticed. In this sense, this is intended to be something of a contemporary meditation "manual," I suppose, a way that will suggest how most of us can go about seeing the depth that is about us, in our very lives, in those we know and love, perhaps even in those we think we hate.*

Too, I am especially fond of people who can converse and chatter almost without end, not that I am totally out of sympathy with the gentleman in one of Jean Kerr's plays, who was driven almost out of his wits by endless gush and gabble, or the affectionate father of one of my German friends who wondered if his offspring would ever shut up. I confess unabashedly my admiration for those who can talk and talk, who can be and are interesting in whatever they say. I am, I confess, a firm believer in Chesterton's remark that there are no uninteresting things, only uninterested people. And while I am most concerned about the condition of silence in our solemn world, probably I envy those persons constantly capable of translating their worlds into words.

"On the way back to St. Louis," a friend wrote to me, "it was a little bumpy in the plane. The sun shines in the window, on my face and shoulders. It feels warm and good. The white clouds look like the snow covered mountains seen in the flight from Boise to Denver. Is this another illusion?" For me, people who can chat about and recount such things seem to have been touched by the fascination and vibrance of our world, about our response to it. The only illusion is that what we see is not there because we do not note it, do not speak about it.

Amid that varied stream of time and place which we discover, in retrospect, has borne us along to where we now are, there is always meaning, and question, and delight, sorrow too. And we do not really see all that we see only by ourselves, at least not totally so. We need to narrate what we see. We are creatures who want to tell the story of where we have been, what we have seen, how we have spoken. Not everyone will be as interested in our many stories as we are ourselves, I suppose. Yet, I find the stories and accounts of my friends to be among the highlights of life. These are what change ideas and abstractions into particularities and details without which things would hardly stand outside of nothingness.

In such a context, we find that men like Marcus Aurelius, men who have lived and wrote centuries before our time, even though Emperors, can still often guide and incite us, both by what they said and what they seemed unaware of. Often I say to my students, after we have read together Plato or Thucydides or Aristotle or Cicero or Marcus Aurelius himself, "Do you not find it strange that such books can still speak directly to each of us, that ancient men often make more sense than those about us?" "What does it tell you about ourselves when we discover that men before our time were wise?" They say, correctly, that human nature must have something constant about it. Our deaths do not mean that our lives will not touch someone down the ages.

Uncannily, in this enterprise, friends, brothers, sisters, companions, those who write to us, who love us, who converse with us, even those who dislike us, become, along with the ancient and famous men and women we may have chanced to have read, the very fabric and stimulus of the chaotic record of *who we are* and of *where we have been*. I do not add of *where we shall go,* since I want that to be a surprise, something I must wait for, because it is part of my choice and part of a universe I did not make.

T. S. Eliot wrote:

> The ordinary man's experience is chaotic, irregular, fragmentary. The latter falls in love, or reads Spinoza, and these two experiences have nothing to do with each other, or with the noise of the typewriter or the smell of cooking; in the mind of the poet these experiences are already forming new wholes.

What I wish to suggest by these meditations is that being a person is also "knowing oneself," also bringing the myriads of things into some reflective purpose and consciousness, into some new whole.

Meditation, it is said, is a conversation with ourselves. I hope this is not wholly so. We converse with ourselves not unmindful of the fact that there is a wide universe about us with fellow human beings who also look out upon this same world, who see it perhaps better than we do, certainly differently, people who tell us about what they too see and mark. A friend once wrote:

> At the present time, things are not quite as hectic, and this helps a little bit. But, on the other hand, I am engaged in "entertainment" — two German ladies are spending their vacation presently with me. One of them will remain here. ... My uncle spent some time with me; other visitors come. And in between, I want to be ALL ALONE! My back has been acting up badly again also — and life goes on. But, by and large, I am enjoying it. There are still many wonderful things, even hot weather can be nice at times.

We are not to be defeated by the chaos. And, as I think, I am a Christian, of sorts. This still means, at a minimum, that our meditations are also hopes that we hear and are heard.

All things, John said in his Prologue, are made in the Word. This means surely that we are to be conscious that all creation speaks to us, along with those who just chat with us, who speak earnestly with us. Could it be that conversation and creation are much the same thing? I think this is mostly so. And so with this, we can begin these musings and wanderings and meditations.

* Though quite different in many ways, my *The Distinctiveness of Christianity* (San Francisco: Ignatius Press, 1983) and, curiously titled, *The Praise of 'Sons of Bitches': On the Worship of God by Fallen Men* (Slough, England: St. Paul Publications, 1978) are perhaps worth noting in this context.

I

To the Gods, I am indebted for having good grandfathers, good parents, a good sister, good teacher, good associates, good kinsmen and friends, nearly everything good.
— *Marcus Aurelius, Meditations, I, 17.*

1. We receive more than we give, even when we give much.

2. Our life is circumscribed by interrupted portions of poignancy and laughter, both. You can know the existence of God from both — the smile and the tear are theological brothers.

3. On the shores of Lake Como, on a blustery spring day, a friend once remarked to me, "I suspect I am more generous than you." This was true, and I am glad of it — not glad that I am not so generous, but that my friends stay with me, even when I cannot easily see why they should, even when they are quite clear about my faults.

4. Lack of power corrupts. Absolute lack of power corrupts absolutely. And yet, weakness is also a hope. Weakness ought not to be chosen, however, but it can be accepted. Strength, too, can be a blessing, much needed.

5. Augustine observed, in his frank way, that the Office of the Roman Emperor was indeed ancient, but that it was filled "by a long succession of dying men." Emperors die and what does it mean to rule an Empire? What does it mean to say that those who are dying rule? Or that those who are ruling die? I have always loved this quotation from Augustine.

6. Of these succeeding, dying men, the most touching, the most poignant was surely Marcus Aurelius. When I was in Rome, each springtime for many years, his wonderful bronze equestrian statue shone green and solemn as I walked through the Campidoglio in the early morning sun. The statue was saved, they say, from zealous Christian idol-smashers because they thought it was Constantine. Two cheers for some errors!

7. There is a legend about this statue. When it begins to turn to gold again, it is said that the world will end. And it was curious, but in the last years when I was in Rome, the statue did seem to be losing its green. The papers wrote articles about it. The statue was not always on the Capitoline Hill, but was moved there by Michelangelo from the Church of John Lateran. Now, it stands silently, majestically, watching the world slowly climb the gently sloping steps before it. Somehow, there always seemed to me to be a sense of gratitude in this Emperor's serene face, in spite of a touch of sadness, too.

Around the corner and down the steps toward the Roman Forum to the left is the Mamartine Prison, where Peter, the Apostle, was once locked up. Peter wrote: "You are slaves of no one except God, so behave like free men, and never use your freedom as an excuse for wickedness. Have respect for everyone and love for your community: fear God and *honor your Emperor*" (I *Peter*, 2:16-17). There is a legend about everlastingness attached to this Peter also.

8. I found a rather good edition of the Stoic Emperor's

Meditations.[1] This was a couple of years ago now. I paid fifty cents for it in a used book store just off Market Street in San Francisco. About every other year, I pull it out and assign it to a class in classical political theory, mainly so I can reread it myself. The students are always struck by these *Meditations*. So am I.

"As for death," I read once in this book, "whether it is dispersion, or dissolution into atoms, or annihilation, it is either extinction or change" (VII, 32). This unsettled me on a late October day in a way that I could not quite define. I did not actually disagree with the great Emperor's alternatives, I suppose. Yet, everything about us presses us to the limits to conceive this change in a hopeful manner.

9. I had a dollar with me. With the other fifty cents, I bought Anne Morrow Lindberg's *Gift from the Sea*, something I had always wanted to read in its entirety. Once I had read a condensed version of *Gift from the Sea* somewhere. It had quieted me. I think that was why I bought it along with the *Meditations* of Marcus Aurelius, a need for calmness. I still have it too, with my Marcus Aurelius.

10. I was going home with myriads of men returning to their own homes after the day's work in San Francisco — along streets, windy, crowded, long successions of dying men, of whom I was one, in the crisp late afternoon. It was the last day of daylight saving time, after which 5 o'clock again becomes 5 o'clock. I began to see the sun go down earlier each day, first disappearing at 5:12, then 5:07, then 4:48, lighting up all in its path, reddening the sky, glowing purple over the Pacific, over the Sundown Sea, as the Indians rightly used to call it, to the West, with unbearable splendor.

1. *Marcus Aurelius and His Times*, Classics Club (Roslyn, New York: Walter J. Black, 1945), containing Marcus Aurelius' *Meditations*, along with writings of Lucan, Justin Martyr, and Walter Pater's essay on the Epicurean.

Buckminster Fuller used to say that it is unscientific and inaccurate to talk about the sun "going down." We should rather say, "the earth is turning." I acknowledge my error — and forget the facts. The sun still goes *down* over the Sundown Sea.

11. So out of my window, over Golden Gate Park, the evening sun went down. Unlike the song, which I tried to sing to myself, I did not hate to see the evening sun go down. I liked to see it go down. About the only dark place in the Universe, after all, the only comfortable one anyhow, is the back side of revolving planets. We are on one of those rare places once a day. We are fortunate, I think.

12. I had a terrible headache, terrible by my standards anyhow. I walked into Golden Gate Park, through the Children's Playground, over to Kirkham Street, then all the way down to Ocean Beach. The waves were very high as was the tide, a low fog hung over the water. It was a stunning sight, really, which I could hardly bear to look at. Pain and beauty exist in the same world, in the same person. I cannot doubt this. I hope pain does not make me doubt beauty. Yet, oftentimes, I have been astonished at how near beauty brings us to pain.

13. My sister, who has had arthritis most of her adult life, wrote, "Being pain-free would surely revolutionize my life. Pain has become a part of me — pain and the effort to avoid it." This is not something I know really. Yet, it is an ultimate question, I think, not pain in general, but pain in our sisters. There is a pain which is not pain when we know it is in those we love.

14. Nikolai Berdyaev wrote: "The mystery of individuality is in every instance revealed only in love, and there is always something in it which is incomprehensible in the last resort and in its final depths."[2]

2. Nikolai Berdyaev, *The Russian Mind* (Boston: Beacon, 1962), p. 1.

If this be true, then, we cannot have so many friends. Aristotle already perceived this and for the same reason. And if we cannot have many friends, if we cannot fully comprehend those we have, then the world is most incomplete at the very place we most want fulfillment. Thus, if we are somehow inexhaustible to others, this is not of our own making. The mystery of individuality is also opaque, even to us, about ourselves. Who am I? How curious is that special day when we first realize that we are the very ones looking out at the world, so full of surprising things. We suddenly realize that "I am the one looking out of myself at what is not me."

15. I said to someone, "You know, the best thing we were ever told by spiritual writers was, not to put our trust in the intellect or upon the passing currents of popular knowledge. We should not be overly perturbed that a Christian view of the world is not a very well accepted one." And yet, the opposite view is also tempting — to cultivate the unpopular *because* it is unpopular. We can become quite weird that way, I suspect.

16. Someone's Law says, "There is no safety in numbers — or in anything else." I think it is Thurber's Law. There is something warm about our plight.

17. Be gentle! Be gentle!

18. In Golden Gate Park one day, a small puppy ran over to two tiny girls. They could not have been more than two; they were playing in the tire swings just after you enter the park from Stanyan Street and Fulton. The puppy licked their faces, then ran off to chase a frisbee its owner had tossed to distract it. The little girls just stood there staring in amazement. It is better that such things exist — the little girls, the puppy, the frisbee, the park, the world.

19. Before she died, my cousin Monica sent me a book. It was a copy of *King Lear*, which had belonged to my own mother. This book was unexpectedly found in my Aunt

5

Josie's belongings. Monica and my mother, who died in 1937, were not too far apart in age.

In the list of characters in the play, there were two left handed check marks (√), one before Edmund, one before Goneril. Edmund says, "This is the excellent foppery of the world, that, when we are sick in fortune — often of the surfeit of our own behaviour — we make guilty of our disasters the sun, the moon, and the stars: as if we were villains on necessity, fools by heavenly compulsion . . ." (Act I, Scene 2).

An eerie feeling this — that one's own mother, who died when you were nine, must have been left-handed, that she too read Shakespeare, once upon a time, that by checking Edmund, she reminded her son many years later of our foibles and pretenses, of his own, even. That left-handed check is, I think, the only thing I possess indicating my mother's mind. Photos, of which I have a few, do not do this. No letters, no words survive. Those who loved us disappear silently.

20. All evening it had been raining. During a lull, I walked over to the corner of the University of San Francisco campus, by Campion Hall, to watch the marvelous lights on Mount Parnassus across the way. Suddenly it began to pour. I rushed back across the campus getting quite soaked.

I went into our coffee room to dry out a bit. An elderly priest friend was sitting there by himself drinking a beer. He looked up at me and out of his own thoughts mused, "You know, I was just thinking of all the old songs I used to know and the people I used to enjoy them with." Loves and lives I could not even imagine suddenly flashed into my mind as I nodded — things incomprehensible, in the last resort. Somehow I felt helpless.

"It is like that when we grow older," I weakly murmured, somehow trying to suppress a wave of tenderness for the old man and his memories. Foolishly, I did not ask him, "What songs?" I think I should like to know some of them now. Music does not die. He was right. He is himself dead now.

21. I once had a little friend of five. Her great aunt and uncle were visiting her. At lunch one day, she told her aunt that she loved her very much. Then, according to her mother, she proceeded to list in order of importance her favorite people.

Here is the list: "Jim Schall, Aunt Marion, God, Aunt Gail, Grandmother, Uncle Ted, and my parents."

Her mother continued, "We all laughed so hard, and then she said, "Well, sorry, that's the way it is."

There is something rather special about outranking God and Aunt Marion in a little girl's affections when she was five. One of the things I believe about both God and Aunt Marion is that they do not mind.

22. During his memorable journey to the Hebrides, in a wonderful book I found someplace, Samuel Johnson remarked, "We could have been easily persuaded to a longer stay upon *Inch Kenneth*, but life will not be all passed in delight." Is this why beauty approaches pain? Somewhere within us, however, is the faint certainty that it all should so be passed in delight. Are these the songs we remember in the evening?

23. A friend who had once broken her leg wrote: "One line of your last letter I loved, 'You are undoubtedly back up on your highly undependable feet again.' Yes, with only an occasional twinge to remind me of some unremembered folly. Isn't it sad not even to acknowledge our follies? Meanwhile, Happy November — elections, football, turkeys, days too short (like life . . .)."

Somehow, this passage almost paralyzed me with sadness. For I love short days. And I believe that when we are called, it is a grace. Yet life is too short, however little we might like to live until we are 135 years old. We are given too much, so many unremembered follies, twinges. Were there more, we could not bear them.

24. A student of mine, an Irishman, once became a Buddhist. He insisted on talking about his new enthusiasm at every occasion. Buddhism is probably great. But it does not especially appeal to me. In fact, I resent being preached at. (How often do I do the same thing, I wonder?)

And yet, I would hate to think that I already know so much that I cannot discover a new way. So I read the paper of my young friend's sect. He was an editor of it, in fact. It was gibberish. I could not understand most of it. But when he asked me how I liked his paper, I lied. "It was helpful. It was interesting." Why is it I love my own enthusiasms, but cannot bear those of others? Still, gibberish is gibberish. Probably that is why.

25. To disagree is the greatest of virtues when done politely. I myself dislike disagreeing. I like to think that mine is a form of virtue. But it is not, at least not always. At worst it is a kind of haughtiness, at best a kind of tolerance. But I love people who can argue and debate.

26. Does this mean that politeness and gentleness are virtues transcending all others? Gentility is a mark of high respect, of great sensibility. We tend to undervalue manners because we believe that they are too easily corrupted into a superiority complex, into a contempt for the rude and the simple.

Yet, civility and gentility are the hope we have of living together. What causes so much confusion is that there are so many codes of manners. It is easy to think that our neighbors are foolish. This is because they often are. But the Sabbath is for man. So are manners. We need both the Sabbath and the manners. The latter without the former is very dangerous because we tend to make our manners our faith if our faith grows cold.

27. If a man is dying, he deserves good medical care. He had good medical care. Still he is dying.

His friends believe that the doctor is not doing all that

can be done because the man is dying. Therefore, they say to the dying man, "Go out and find a good doctor."

He goes out and finds another doctor. Still he is dying. The first doctor is angry because his reputation is challenged. To be sure, there are quite a few incompetent and inattentive physicians. And to have a doctor at all is a blessing and an evolution and sometimes a nuisance. Not everyone has a doctor in this world.

Requiescat in Pace. May he rest in peace. My friend died. In none of this advice to change doctors was there any intent to be other than helpful and responsible and concerned. Indeed, there is something out of whack at the center of our lives. By trying to help, often we make things worse. Why is the world like this?

28. I read this astounding proclamation: "Every Human Being Has an Absolute Right to His Own Individual Happiness." God made the world, I think, so that we do not and cannot have such an *absolute right*. Our individual happiness is a gift, not a right. It is something of our own making only in the most restricted sense. Nor is it something that depends on ourselves. If we received happiness as a result of an absolute right, we would receive it as a duty and an obligation, even as a coercion.

To have an absolute right to happiness is an absolute guarantee of never receiving happiness. Because it is not our absolute right, it can be really ours, but as a gift.

29. Why does anyone accept a position of responsibility and power? Chesterton said that no one should rule who wanted to rule. Plato said much the same thing. This was said to safeguard the ruled.

Yet, we need authority and decision. We need people who will rule, who will not be crushed by it. President Reagan said that he could not conceive a worse job than his. The ruler is the artist of the future and the conserver of the past. He accepts rule because he sees things can be other-

9

wise. Yet some things that are good are to be kept. The good ruler rules to produce an acceptable otherwise or to prevent a worse kind of environment.

For this reason, we can assume that anyone who rules is within an orbit of danger. We rightly distrust someone who wants to rule too much. Yet, we cannot do without an authority. The only valid title to rule is service. And those who only want to *be* served cannot be ruled.

30. A couple of years ago, I was in Edwards Square in London. It was almost raining, as it often is in England. Lovely Georgian houses surrounded a green, an enclosed park in the center of the square. The house on the corner, my friend showed me, was where Chesterton had lived during part of his London career, before he settled in Beaconsfield, which I also saw later.

This never ceases to amaze me, that men live in a definite place, in definite surroundings, with definite addresses. We arrive there often after their time. We find life has gone on. Other lives are now being lived in these quiet enclaves.

It will be so with us. The claim that we have an *absolute right* to our individual happiness cannot bear the burden of a walk through Edwards Square in London.

Chesterton wrote in 1911, perhaps looking out on the very green I had visited: "You cannot have too much of a good thing, which is the chief demonstration of the doctrine of everlasting life."[3]

How utterly sad it is to claim as an absolute right our own happiness. The beginning of everlasting life is the discovery of one good thing to which we have no right. You cannot indeed have too much of a good thing.

31. We can give because we have received.

32. Absolute corruption results from the "absolute happiness" to which we have an absolute right.

33. Mercy is more profound than justice because we

3. G. K. Chesterton, *Lunacy and Letters*, p. 175.

have no right to it. After we read together from John Rawls'
A Theory of Justice, which tried to outline a system of perfect justice, I said to my class, "A society of perfect justice
would be a hell." They looked at me.

34. Enthusiasm is always at the border of madness. The
new way, the new vision, will make everyone happy, content, and loving. This is what we are told.

For me, however, I like my enthusiasms tinged with a
little sadness, tempered with the realization that we are all
obnoxious at times, that things are not just fine when they
are not in fact just fine, even if we do not say so because we
are polite.

35. In a Russian Exhibit in the de Young Museum in
Golden Gate Park, there are many lovely Byzantine-rite
icons. An icon has a theology behind it, the divine light
breaks through it. I admit that things can break through the
structure of the world. And I am glad of it.

36. A friend wrote, "I am glad you believe in the 'infinity and mystery stuff' of each human person. You may be
surprised to know that I didn't know I believed in that stuff
until you wrote about it. I always did believe it, but did not
know I did. That makes little sense, does it? Ah, well. . . ."
Knowing what we do not know we know is what fullness of
life is about. We are beings meant to illuminate *what is*, including the mystery of each human person. "Stuff" is sometimes the best word.

37. I believe mainly because there is no other way to
explain the fact of laughter, not the theory of laughter, but
the fact. Yet, I often feel that laughter, at least its abundance in our lives, is somehow a gift following on belief.
Laughter is the sign *not* of the capacity to forgive, but of the
fact of having already been forgiven, of being able to forgive
what ought not to have been.

38. Pete, Mike, and I went over one cloudy evening to
dinner at my brother's. On the way home, across the Bay
Bridge, Pete, who had never met him before, said: "I have

the feeling that your brother has never met a stranger." That is one of those things I have always known about my brother, but never realized it before. Both of my brothers, in fact, are like this.

39. We have a tomorrow to anticipate, and our world, we are told, is full of doom. Marcus Aurelius knew that he was indebted for his family, his friends, for nearly everything that was good. Are we doomed even if we are doomed to die?

Not even our relation to God is one of indebtedness. For we are related to one another, and to the divinity, but not through justice. In the beginning, we need not be. And we are. I am.

II

*You see how few the things are which a man needs to
lay hold of in order to live a life which flows in quiet,
and is like the life of the gods. . . .*
— *Marcus Aurelius, Meditations, II, 5.*

1. Each of us can begin something that has never been begun before. The improbable is possible. This is our freedom.

2. We cannot and should not live our whole lives in privacy. But there is no civilization, no personality even, without locked doors.

3. The story is told of Pope John XXIII patiently listening to someone at an official function addressing him in flowing speech — "Most Holy Father," "Beatissimo Papa," and so on. The old Pope heard it all with a smile.

At the end, he rose, raised his arms, and said to the crowd, merely "Coraggio!" (Have courage about it all!) Everyone cheered. For it is no small thing to be told by a Pope simply to have courage through it all, the boredoms of our lives. Courage was once a military virtue. Today, it seems, it is needed merely to get through the day.

4. A columnist in the morning newspaper, McCabe perhaps, once spoke of burning the works of Zane Grey. He did not like them. The main vice in cowboy stories is vengeance.

13

Nothing is forgiven. Justice is done. This is their story, their drama. Justice frightens men. Rightly so.

5. In the Epilogue of *The Tempest*, Prospero sang:

Now I want
Spirits to enforce, art to enchant:
And my ending — is despair,
Unless I be retrieved by prayer
Which pierces so, that it assaults
Mercy itself, and frees all faults.

Coraggio, vengeance, justice — faults are freed through mercy and prayer. Ultimately, there are no technical solutions. Mercy can pierce despair. *Coraggio*.

6. We cannot have many friends. Most will think this is a sadness. And it is, in a way. But on the whole, it is a freedom. If we really are mysteries, we should not expect a lifetime to be too long, even for one or two others.

7. There was a heavy fog over Frank's Tract, a large, submerged acreage of land along the Sacramento River Delta. Many boats were floating at anchor with us. My brother and I were fishing, catching nothing, but with a few bites to make it interesting.

Fishing is a symbol of unexpectedness. Something might just happen at any moment; then again, it may not. Either way, we cruised home, refreshed, having learned again to expect, to be content with catching nothing.

8 "What do you think about when you are fishing?" Ann asked years later. "You think about fishing," I said. "Absolutely boring," she said. "You cannot be a Christian," I replied, "if you cannot understand the fascination of fishing." "You cannot be a Christian if you cannot understand the fascination of knitting," she replied. "Knitting is boring," I said. "We both either need to know how to knit or fish, or change our theories," was the just reply.

9. "There are some questions to which there are no answers and others which are not yet ripe for answers."

"Mull that over!"

The trouble is, of course, that we are not ever sure which is which, the no answers and the no answers yet. Yet, it is so. It is a relief not to have answers to all questions. And still we anticipate. Our condition bids us to wait. And this too is a grace.

10. Stoicism strove for inner peace, even against the turmoil of the world outside. But we want the world outside to break into our interior peace sometimes. Otherwise, our world would be too small.

11. Also in the de Young Museum in Golden Gate Park, there hangs a huge painting of Francis of Assisi, alone, at prayer in a cave. The painter was El Greco himself. Francis is meditating before a Crucifix. His face is young, mild, absorbed. I walked over to see this painting again this afternoon, midst the late autumn sun, the green of the park.

Beauty and mystery are all about us. We need not always have to go someplace else to find them.

12. A city is full of a variety of people, lives, so many we shall never see again as we pass them by. There they are, myriads of cross sections of mankind and myriads of cross purposes. The city is man's greatest human invention, I think. There are greater institutions, but they are not man's.

13. The tide was far out on Ocean Beach. As I walked along, down by the far end of the park, three girls were sitting cross-legged, Buddhist-style, praying, presumably, facing the bright sun, the sea, the waves. Not to pray before such a view would be, in fact, abnormal.

14. All day I was expecting someone. No one came. Life goes on. Disappointments are also gifts.

15. P. G. Wodehouse's *Joy in the Morning* says, "If there's one thing the Woosters are, it's fairminded. We

writhe, but we are just." This is perfect. There is no way to make justice easy, or even very attractive. Indeed, there may be no way to make it even possible.

16. "It is well-known that the world, as portrayed in the press, is a worse place than the world in which men live, because all the accidents, all the antagonisms, all the underlying strains and tensions, all the problems and threats, can make news, where the placidity of daily life, which is the main preoccupation of most of the human race, is of little use to the news media." Douglas Woodruff wrote this in *The Tablet* in London on November 4, 1972.

I believe, however, that ordinariness can often be quite thrilling.

17. Everyone has a natural right to feel lousy, sometimes.

18. Should there be no absolute person against whom to measure ourselves, we would cease to be. The opposite of this seems to be also true. If there be such an absolute person, there is no way to make us uninteresting. This is why the history of vice and the history of virtue both have their abiding fascination, even when both happen to the same person, as they usually do.

19. Boredom seems ridiculous to me. But I am fortunate in friends and places. Yet, I wonder if it can be reduced to this. I believe all the essential drama of our existence is played out wherever two or three are gathered together. And we are given so much more than just the bare, essential drama. The great mystery is not why are we given so little, but why we are given so much.

20. In Bunuel's film, "Simon of the Desert," all the drama of heaven and earth are in the desert and in the city. Holiness consists of being odd. So does unholiness. There is no escape. *Coraggio*.

Helen Waddell in her *Desert Fathers* wondered what these odd gentlemen bequeathed to us. "Yet one intellectual concept they did give to Europe: eternity . . . These men, by the very exaggeration of their lives, stamped infinity on the imagination of the West. They saw the life of the body as Paulinus saw it, 'occidui temporis umbra,' a shadow at sunset. 'The spaces of our human life set over against eternity' — it is the undercurrent of all Anthony's thought — 'are most brief and poor.' "

Marcus Aurelius would have understood that, the shadow at sunset. It was to escape from his Empire that the monks went into the desert.

21. The disturbing thing about Christianity in the twentieth century is not that it has been "refuted" and shown therefore barren. The disturbing thing is that it has proven to be barren for so many, but is yet to be refuted. The barrenness has other, more spiritual sources. The first to notice when Christians lose their faith and their zeal are those who would hope this faith to be true.

22. In *A Thousand Clowns*, it is stated: "That's the most you should expect of life, Sandy, a really good apology for all the things you won't get." This is true. Nonetheless, the things we won't get should not drive us mad. They are graces too, no doubt. No one needs to apologize, not even life. For most of the great things that ever will happen, we shall, mostly, not be present. So be it. Still all that we need, we have. Do not be bored. It may be the deadliest sin.

23. We need solemnity. However, solemnity is not a need. It is a response. To walk slowly about the Altar is not just a rubric. It is an awe.

24. Christianity is the religion of *re*-joicing, of enjoying *again*. To be a Christian is to refuse to believe that joy is exhausted in the experience of enjoying. Joy is the most solemn of experiences because it brings us nearest to the Divinity. Joy always disturbs us because it contains within its very experience a promise. The second coming is the necessary condition of joy *to* and *in* the world.

"Rejoice," Paul said, "again, I say, rejoice" — almost as if the very word itself has to be repeated.

17

25. A crowded street in a city is a good symbol of our common lot — faces, lives we could perhaps know, but never will. Yet, we realize there is drama everywhere. It takes our life merely to plot our own, one life, one drama for each of us.

26. The improbable is possible, that is why we exist. Therefore, when we exist, everything about us in the world is full of unlikelihoods. Enjoy them! Praise them!

27. Psalm 149 says, "Let them praise his name with dancing, making melody to the timbrel and lyre." If this seems like an odd way to praise God, it is because our notion of God is probably quite odd. Let God tell us who he is, rather than suppose that our picture of him is adequate or complete.

28. In Gene Fowler's biography of Jimmy Durante, there is an especially wonderful passage I like: "Lately, the Schnozzola has been wearing horn-rimmed spectacles, but he says, 'I think I'll quit putting on my glasses, because everybody looks so beautiful the other way.' " I do not suppose Durante meant that the world was ugly if you could see it as it is. He was more simple and straightforward.

Blurry things are beautiful too — and I often think that the blurriness of things, all things, is deliberate. We could not really bear their real loveliness.

29. We also walk slowly with our friends because we do not want to get where we are going, for we are already there if they are our friends. One of the definitions of dancing, I think, is that it is what you do when you arrive at where you want to be.

30. Once I sent to friends, on a whim, an amusing newspaper photo of the Italian Army Chaplain Corps after the Ethiopian War, marching in formation, each wearing a cassock and battle ribbons, before the Monumento Vittore Emanuele in the Piazza Venezia. As a present, I received it back in a couple of days, unexpectedly, this time reproduced and mounted as a picture. A passing fancy became permanent because friends created something that never existed

before. The sum total of reality became somehow greater. I still have it.

31. The mystery of divine providence is not that it is grim and vindicative, but that it is humorous and mild. Why do the just suffer? Why can believers laugh? Somehow, the answers to these questions involve each other.

32. What prevents the turnings of the earth, the years, from being eternally the same is memory, the fact that on this or that turning, something happened to men or women or usually both who were living in this place or that. What is passed on is both the commonness of our lives and their uniqueness, both.

33. Politeness and manners. — These seem again the most essential elements of culture. And there are many forms of politeness, many kinds of manners, though they must, it strikes me, show a graciousness and a kindness. So without some attention to manners, life is mostly defeated. I believe one of Flannery O'Connor's books was called, *Mystery and Manners*. The great revolutions may well be those in which we learn to tip our hats to a lady or invite our guests into our homes, *after* they knock.

34. The wind was blowing quite strongly in San Francisco. It was the day after Christmas. The wind had cleared the green, barren hills. New things begin when old things are remembered.

35. Everyone has something to offer someone else. We learn what we can up to a point. Then we pass on to other topics. We never exhaust what there is, probably, as Aquinas said, because it is. I learned this from reading Aquinas. I have a friend who learned it from just living.

36. Giving up things is also an act of judgment. This is why it is hard to be ascetic. In a way, the instinct to indulgence is more healthy because it is a sign of human weakness and, therefore, of humanity itself. It is also somehow a sign of the abundance of things, a sense that God is "diffusive" of himself, as Aquinas also said.

II

37. The few things we need to be satisfied should be sought out and accepted. Yet, the abundance of the universe is not to be conceived as somehow a sort of divine trap, better not given at all. How little we need is one of the great wonders of our species. How much there is given is another.

III

Men know not how many things are signified by the words stealing, sowing, buying, keeping the peace, seeing what ought to be done; for this cannot be done by the eyes, but by another kind of vision.
– Marcus Aurelius, Meditations, III, 15.

1. On my return, Rome was beautiful. Spring was late. Soon after my settling in, over on Monte Mario, I saw my first flowering plum blossoms, purple in the afternoon sun, the city stretched out below, magnificent, ancient, warm, eternal, one of the places our thoughts must somehow reckon with.

2. Things keep slipping away. Familiar persons are now gone, to be about their lives. In this existence, we are given much, but things do not happen all at once. Little changes take place. Gradually, our memories create the place we were in, how we looked at it.

3. "What do you expect of life?" I asked a friend, with no particular intention to be profound. "I have received so much more than I ever expected of life that I live in a constant state of 'touching wood' so to speak. And yet, when you say, 'What do you expect of life?'—the answer is 'More'."

4. Is it possible to have a better world? In Mexico, on

21

the way over to Rome one year, I learned, visiting my friend Tom Conn in Jalapa, that the drama of life and grace is present even in the poorest place. Our spiritual lives and their depth cannot be reduced to our material circumstances. The shattering presence of the love of God and of one another is everywhere. No one is closer or farther away. This is the real danger of the rich and the clerics who say they are "working for the poor." They often seem to imply that, unless they do, God will somehow not be there already. This is why John Paul II says, "Teach spiritual things first, then these things will be added unto you."

5. One Holy Thursday, I was walking along the ancient battlements of Verona in Northern Italy. Those military walls and mounds are now a quiet park with flowers and blossoms in full springtime beauty. As I walked along, a little girl combed her mother's hair. Somewhat farther into the park, little boys were busily playing war. They charged down the hill with their pistols, rifles and toy hand grenades. Suddenly, they fell over and rolled down, dead.

6. Not far from the great Church of Saint Zeno in Verona was an Italian War Memorial. It listed the wars and defeats and victories of the Italians for a hundred years. The little boys, who, as men, actually fell down and rolled over; were they once here also, like the little boys I saw? The city is where we remember our dead and through them, where men have been. Too, it is a place where battlements become monuments and parks for boys to play in, for little girls to comb their mother's hair.

7. Style is a dangerous virtue, but it is a virtue. Christianity holds, in some obscure way, that we were all intended *to be* and intended to be the human persons we are. Style is that sense of individuality and personality that seeks to make the very best of the very best thing about — *what we are*. The close relationship of style and clothing is

not accidental. The Greeks even made, in their logic, "style," *habitus*, a special relationship, how we add to ourselves.

8. At a lovely concert in Saint Euphemia on Good Friday in Verona, they sang parts of the Bach *Saint Matthew Passion*, while they read other sections of the Passion, a "spiritual concert." The young man in front of me talked all during this magnificent, solemn setting. He prevented his young lady friends from listening. He did not listen himself. He seemed a very shallow young man to me. You cannot hear Bach and talk, especially if you are there to reflect on the Passion according to Saint Matthew on Good Friday.

Liturgy should, at times, be silent, solemn, no applause, no talking. Everyone has an interior he or she must discover and retain. Yet, I suppose, lives have different convergences — talking to young ladies, after all, is hardly an indefensible enterprise for a young man.

9. There was a production of Celine's *L'Eglise*, in Paris, which the *Herald-Tribune's* T. Q. Curtiss reported in this way: "The lengthy tale of sound and fury concludes with the message that life's meaning is beyond the imagination of man." And I hope this is true. For life's meaning *not* to be beyond man's imagination would be a kind of imprisonment, I should think.

10. Gardone is a small resort town along Lake Garda in Northern Italy. In the morning when I was there, early, there was no one along its beautiful walk beside the water. Haze obscured the sun and mountains. It was pleasant to sit there in silence, half way absorbed in it all, reading a newspaper, reflecting on the world, yet retaining a certain self-awareness and possession. All of man's problems are our own personal problems in a way.

Yet, through it all, we must be able merely to sit at times and really to be content in spite of whatever is going on in the vast world. There is a Marxist splinter group in Italy which called itself "Lotta Continua" — continual struggle. I have often thought they must be very unhappy people who look out on the world in such a way. They would say, no doubt, that the world leaves no other choice. But that is the only choice they leave the world.

11. Not all of our pleasures are complete. Sometimes, they cannot be completed. Still, even a minimum of delight is oftentimes more than we might expect. I often feel that unlimited expectations are the cause of our failure to appreciate what we do receive. But we do have unlimited expectations. How do the two fit together? That is indeed the wonder.

12. Sometimes we merely receive, unable to give back. This often approaches the highest moments of our existence. We should not disdain our limitations.

13. "You are a very comfortable person," someone told me. This, of course, is hardly a compliment among the revolutionaries and the flaky. Comfort — my old dictionary said it sometimes is spelled, "cumfort" — means this:

> In this sense, comfort is more solid than amusements, more quiet and stable than pleasure, less positive and vivid than happiness. One lives in comfort who has a sufficiency of those things which meet the immediate and natural demands of body and mind, so as to minister to contentment and tranquil enjoyment. Comfort may also be used of any relief under suffering, want, or sorrow, which makes the distress easier to be borne.

In my own mind, I associate "comfortable" mainly with the idea of home, of a place to which, in the end, we return to, if we are so fortunate.

14. There is a difference between passion and affection. They are related, but they are not the same.

15. We are a tragic race. And this is true as much of our comforts, passions, and affections as it is of our unexpected,

unjust, unwanted deaths. But we are also a funny race. It is often difficult to know which is more problematic to come to terms with — the fact that we die or the fact that we laugh. I am inclined to suspect the latter.

16. A friend wrote: "Sometimes I read the last page of a book before I start it. Impatient and not wanting to wait, knowing where you are going before you take the step. I know now that I will love the book because the last page is perfect. Just perfect. 'Concrete joys keep us unbalanced because we keep running into them.' How sweet it is." I had forgotten about the concrete joys, the only kind that there are, the kind we keep running into.

17. They say that if we are content and comfortable in our lives, that we shall never do a great, noble thing. I like what the late Charles McCabe wrote once in the *San Francisco Chronicle:*

> I do not know the exact hour that I gave up on perfection, but it was the best hour of my life. There comes a point when, if you have the luck and the wit, you realize that you are what you are. That, too, is a cliché, but when the truth of it comes to you with all its feral force, you know what life has in store for you.
>
> That is: the chance to know yourself more fully, and nothing more. No writing of epics or constitutions, no leading of charges or landings on moons; nothing more than a protracted and in the end thrilling examination of conscience.

Yet, in all of this, noble and great things are usually done that the rest of us can find peace and comfort, so that we can be at home in the early dusk of an evening.

19. Without condoning all, without lapsing into a kind of relativism that refuses to see any real differences between things and principles and people, I suspect nonethe-

less that it is true that most of the really good deeds men do to one another, most of the really good people that do live on this earth, go simply unrecognized and unnoticed.

There are different kinds of visions. Marcus Aurelius was right.

IV

Men seek retreats for themselves, houses in the country, seashores, and mountains; and you are wont to desire such things very much. But this is altogether a mark of the common sort of man, for it is in your power, whenever you choose, to retire into yourself.
– Marcus Aurelius, Meditations, IV, 3.

1. It was autumn again in San Francisco. Friendship is most difficult because it does not in fact last, at least not in the way we thought it would, swore it would, when we were younger. Aristotle already noted this in the *Ethics*, but he is hard to believe when we are young. I can see it in the eyes of the young students when they read his passages talking about themselves. We change. Our friends change. Friends must grow proportionately together, though perhaps not in the same ways. And when we or our friends take certain options, certain choices, we can no longer abide with them, since friendship is primarily a sharing of truth and goodness. The ancients were mostly right. If by the time we reach fifty, we have two or three friends, we are lucky.

2. Music and politics are closer than we think. Plato and Aristotle knew this. Every absolutist government in the world today takes this for granted. The Polish conductor

visiting San Francisco said that the freedom to give a new performance of something old is at the heart of true liberty.

3. Sentiment is hard to bear. Life is action and must go on. We cannot spend our time in memory and might-have-beens. Nevertheless, never to remember is shallowness. Our hearts are restless because they have rested, because they have once known peace and affection. And what might-have-been truly might-have-been. Our lives might have been otherwise.

4. Propriety is a necessary quality. There are so many things that are ethically all right to do but which are nonetheless improper. Even the good requires proportion. Manners, everyone knows, can be tyrants, only less so than the lack of them. But manners are the essence of mutual respect. The contemporary attack on them, their studied neglect, is a gradual reversal to barbarism.

5. In Boswell's dedication of his *Life of Samuel Johnson*, to Sir Joshua Reynolds, he says, "And though I tell nothing but the truth, I have still kept in my mind that the whole truth is not always to be exposed." This is most proper and accurate, part of the very being of our freedom.

If the very definition of friendship, or at least its context, is that friends are to have "all things in common," as Plato suggested in *The Republic*, much to the amazement of the young listeners, it also implies that everything is in common exclusively to the friends alone. Intensity of feeling can be public. But this is not all there is to our feelings. Mystery and meaning remain hidden, even from ourselves at times. This is why Boswell went on to say that he loved the *Journey to the Western Islands*, but still wished that "a few of our hero's foibles had been a little more shaded."

Our friends need to bear with our faults, but they need not be put on display. I would prefer not to know the sins of my friends, or of myself, for that matter, though the latter is rather more difficult in the nature of things.

6. "Our eldest son grew more nostalgic as the program

progressed and finally said he couldn't bear it. 'Why, why did we leave Italy?' They are all terribly homesick, and when it strikes one that they are homesick for the wrong place, I must remind myself that after all, Italy is all they knew." — Homesickness for the wrong place: I suspect this is close to the definition of the human condition.

7. Andrew Wyeth said — I saw this on the wall at his Exhibit in the de Young Museum — that the good is a little terrifying and a little sad too.

Yes, I think that the good takes improbable forms and cannot be totally suppressed. Sometimes, you suddenly meet people who are good, and this is very disarming. The good is a little sad too. At first, I should not be prepared to accept this. Yet, I am a Christian, that is, someone who knows of the Cross.

8. Nevertheless, I retorted, "I do not believe in the sinlessness of eighteen-year-olds" — this in response to a young man who was passionately angered at the conduct of the then Vice-President and at the government for his light sentence. He himself was trying to live a good life, the young man said.

This is why, I suppose, young men are incapable of really studying ethics, as Aristotle said. They lack experience and insight into what they themselves have done. They cannot yet imagine what they will do, they and those they love.

9. *The Annals* of Tacitus were a marvel and a horror, too, of moral history. "The report of the surrender and kind reception of Segestes, when generally known, was heard with hope or grief according as men shrank from war or desired it" (I, 59). There is a clear insight here into the nature of subjectivity and objectivity. We so often do control what we see that our vision ever can be a function of our choice.

10. In the Gospel of *Mark*, there is the story of how the Lord came to establish a new kind of rule, one in which

29

serving, not being served, was the title to rule. In a sense, all authority since then has gradually been infiltrated by this criterion. The passage in *Mark* ends by saying that the Son of Man came to give his life as a ransom for many—for all, really (10:41-45).

The great Christian challenge is that we cannot ultimately really rule ourselves unless we first accept this service, this sacrifice that someone else was lost so that we might live. This ought to be the first meditation for all who rule, that their lives are to be given as a ransom for many.

11. All men that have so far lived on earth — some eighty or ninety billions, they say — have lived in some sort of vale of tears. This is a fact, even though the vale may be better or worse. And yet, we are haunted by the dream that this need not be so. Many would even hold that this belief in a possibility of improvement, radical improvement, alone can cause improvement.

But the dream of actually escaping the valley of tears is probably itself the cause of most of our inability to appreciate and confront the things that are given to us and of our inability to change the things we can change. In his book, *Political Philosophy and the Open Society*, Dante Germino rightly worries about the ultimate fate of our kind, its openness to transcendence.[4] He is right.

12. Walking through a small park off Arguello Street in San Francisco, I passed a young woman carrying a very tiny baby in a sack-like arrangement slung over her neck. She was sitting on the stoop of the gate into the Park. I nodded. She responded in a very flat, nasal, broad-accented, perhaps Texan, "Howdy." Her intonation amused me. Perhaps life is not so complicated after all, at least about basic things. Strange how much kindness the tone of the human voice can

4. Dante Germino, *Political Philosophy and the Open Society* (Baton Rouge: Louisiana State University Press, 1982).

carry, even when it just says, "Howdy."

13. Back in 1973, I had been invited to a conference in New Zealand. While at a lovely seminary-farm near Hawke's Bay on the North Island, someone gave me a copy of James K. Baxter's poems. He wrote, in one of his peculiarly titled, "Pig Island Letters":

> For me it is the weirs that mention
> The love that we destroy
> By long evasion, politics and art,
> And speech that is a kind of contraception:
> A street light flashing down
> On muscled water, bodies in the shade,
> Tears on a moonwhite face, the voice
> Of time from the grave of water speaking to
> Those who are lucky to be sad.

That last line is a very haunting one — "Those who are lucky to be sad." Just how is one to understand this? That those who are unfeeling miss much? That our pains are a sign of our existence? That we live in a world in which sadness portends that we are destined for happiness? Our sadness, it seems, is connected with the sort of being we have been given.

14. My sister wrote: "In fact, I am getting now to where I do not trust pain as a signal of something important. I do not always like myself so much, but that is a vicious circle. Usually the reason is that I hate me for feeling pain so much, and then for not being able to 'go on' in spite of pain." I have never thought of such a possibility — of not liking oneself because of the body I have been given, though when my eyes hurt, I almost do. That is one of the privileges of generally good health, I suppose. The Feast of Our Lady of Sorrows is September 15. In the liturgy, we forget, is this realization that pain and sadness are part of our lot, that we must reckon with them, as the Scripture tells us. I read the

words of my sister to the others. How much more does she know than I? — so I thought to myself later.

15. In Iris Murdoch's *Accidental Man*, I read: "Only youth preserves some illusions of radiance because the ability to be surprised has not yet worn away."

"I hope this is not so true," I wrote to a friend, like myself no longer a youth.

16. I watched the end of the World Series on television. It was the famous day on which there is no tomorrow. I love contests in which there is and must be a winner and a loser. After the series, the winning team was falling apart. The manager was fighting with the irascible owner. It is well to see that something is at stake, that accidents are part of our accomplishments as well as of our skills. The end of the season, autumn. It is a reflective time, to realize that we are in a world that remains the same, yet changes too, that championships are decided, to be played again next year.

17. A fall evening in San Francisco, mild, beautiful, a Sunday — the world changes. Msgr. John Tracy Ellis had invited me to dinner downtown, over on the other side of Nob Hill. We took the bus to Market Street, but decided to walk to Powell and Washington Street.

Strange reactions, funny incidents, when two men in Roman collars and black suits walk by. As we passed the first movie house specializing in X-rated features, no way to avoid, the barker in the street blandly invited us in — "Only a Dollar." Msgr. Ellis was nonplussed.

From across the street, a drunk, well-dressed, came stumbling down Jones Street — "Hello, Fathers." He was obviously one of the flock, but he was too tanked even to get this out clearly. We then passed three young blacks in the most outlandishly beautiful suits, one a luminous pink job with a white broad-rimmed hat. They stared at us as if somehow *we* had come up with a more striking uniform.

There was a long line of youngsters on Sutter Street

waiting to get into the New Boarding House for a rock concert. Walking back on Mason Street, we passed two convention-attending ladies, both quite smashed. The Monsignor, historian that he is, paused to comment on the decline of civilization. Two other young ladies wanted to know the time. They seemed to me uncomfortably like ladies of the night. A young man then tapped me on the shoulder and wanted us to come to a "Buddhist Prayer Meeting."

By the time we finally climbed into the Geary Street Bus, I decided that no walk I had taken lately so graphically showed how much the world has been changing. Symbols like the Roman collar do not mean the same things any more. There is a total chaos and diversity of basic assumptions. This is the world we live in.

18. R. H. Tawney once gave a lecture (December 9, 1952) at the University of London, in which he said of the Webbs:

> It is sufficient to say that the inhuman doctrinaires of the journalistic legend were known to their friends as two sociable people, with a psychological curiosity not too elevated to enjoy gossip, an engaging capacity for laughing at themselves, and an attitude towards their fellow-travellers in this vale of tears which, if at times left the tortoises a little breathless, was in general that expressed in the remark of one of the partners that, of all forms of happiness, companionship is the most delightful.

I found this reprint on a windy, rainy night in October, a night which itself made me feel cozy and content, but there were no companions in sight.

Sometimes, I think companionship makes us miss the wind and the rain, but the Webbs were mostly right on this point, if we assume, that is, that we really do know the forms in which happiness might indeed appear to us. That we do not know this fully, this is what revelation seems to be mostly about.

19. A friend wrote from Africa:

> I am still playing tennis, but everybody is kind of giving up on me. Guess I'll go back to playing against the wall. You know what I like best about tennis? to sit around after the game and shoot the breeze. I really like that. I just don't like the idea of tennis being work. I want to play and have fun and enjoy myself. But there are people who don't have the same ideas as I have.

I wrote back that when you play, play to win. But I doubt if it will help. My friend's ideas are much too metaphysical in the end.

20. "I'm a fatalist in a way," my brother told me, as we were in a commuter bus crossing the Bay Bridge in the early evening. "You cannot really rely on doctors or medicine for everything." This is surely correct. Our sister or my brother's wife, with much pain even after seeing years of doctors and tons of pills, both forbid any other conclusion. Ultimately, I think, we are good judges of ourselves and our own health, not in any infallible way, but we know when something hurts. Plato would have agreed, I think.

Still, as our sister said, sometimes even pain cannot be trusted. Christianity in its mystery maintains somehow that pain is redemptive. How different it seems if it is. Still, the pain, the suffering, remains. We are not told it will be otherwise, in spite of all the utopian promises which so charge our world.

21. "Love to me is giving and sharing of all feelings, accepting the problems and anxieties that accompany that love. So many don't know how to give, or receive, for that matter." This is probably why love is not merely a joy but a

suffering and an anguish too, why it can be as frightening as it is joyous.

And yet, it is joyous. The difficulty of receiving is love's greatest paradox.

22. Loneliness is an intrinsic aspect of healthy personality. There is and must be in all of us somewhere an interior, deep loneliness. We cannot escape this. Small groups, deep loves, comradeship, companionship, activity, all of these, good and necessary though they be, will never erase the basic loneliness that is also about us.

Loneliness, then, is the sign that we are never satisfied with any earthly love or work, a sign of the dignity of our creation. This too is why we must be somewhat skeptical about all enthusiasms and friendships which are conceived in terms of removing this fundamental loneliness. Should they succeed, they can only end up by making our lives more shallow. We are made for something else, yet this too.

23. I was invited to help a friend celebrate a military promotion, to lieutenant colonel. He sent an invitation. The notion of an invitation is a most essential thing we must have in our relationships with others. There are some things we can only be invited to, things we cannot demand, or force, or insist on.

We are thus powerless before things which can only be shared through invitation. It seems odd that our friendships as well as our destiny can only be achieved through invitation, possibly because our destiny is also a friendship. For this reason, too, we must respect rigidly and carefully those things into which we are not invited. The privacy of others is but the counter of our own.

24. Gabriel Marcel died some years ago now. When he did pass away, I felt that I must read something of this gentle, meditative man. In his *Man Against Mass Society*, I read:

One might pursue similar reflections about the

disappearance of the sense of hospitality today, at least in the countries which have been submerged in technical progress. We ought, of course, to be accurate in our way of stating this: To be sure, famous visitors, well-known scholars, writers, or artists are usually very well received in all countries. But by the sense of hospitality, I mean above all that sort of piety which is shown in the East to the unknown guest, because he has entrusted himself to a man and his dwelling.

"John has this quality," I wrote to a friend. The last time I saw him, he simply said, "Welcome home." But it was not my home. Yet, his hospitality made it so for a time.

Loneliness, invitation, and hospitality, all are related somehow. Unexpected hospitality, welcome invitations are portents that our loneliness cannot be our ultimate lot, even while it is the absolute condition of our privacy and our finiteness.

25. "We all need physical attraction in our lives. Such an intensity of feeling makes us warmer, more giving people." The abuse of physical attraction often makes us leery of it. Josef Pieper says that it is the sign or the symbol that no life is secure from the crashing in from the outside of a new life, a new force that breaks us out of our closed-in world. It is always disturbing, often destructive, yet ever there and not meant to be anything less than a force to make us gentler, more giving, warmer people.

26. Horace Gregory's poem stays with me:

> If you would save me,
> Save these lines, these letters,
> Postcards, glazed views of Naples, Nice and Rome.
> They are my life, hopes for a further journey. . . .

Chesterton had remarked that mailing a letter was an irrevocable and, therefore, essentially romantic act. Letters and cards — memories, bits of humor, people we know or want to know. Our links to such things are to further journeys. We travel because we are travelers—*homo viator, homines viatores.* Our letters recall to others that we are on our way, but we want our friends to know this. It is difficult to walk alone, to travel, yet we must sometimes.

27. Saturday was a beautiful, sunny fall day on the shore of Monterey Bay. The tide was low, so we looked for some clams. The constant prodding of the fork in the rough, refreshing surf-mixed sand. The expectation of a good chowder on a cool evening is a pleasure that has no opposite. It is a joy unaccompanied, unaccounted for by any counter pain.

We finally found nine clams, large enough to keep. Each needs to be five inches across. These clams were abundant in the sands of the sea, until they began to protect sea otters. Clams are a life that leaves shells here below the sand, pressed now for millions of years. There are cycles of ages begun long before men, still here, rich to be enjoyed and wondered at. There is nothing more beautiful than a whole clam shell held against the blue horizon. We forget that pure shape is unaccountably beautiful.

How do they ever dig beneath the sand? We know what the science books tell us. That is, we do not really know.

28. Fortitude. — The sermon was on fortitude, persistence. There will ever be struggle, conflict. We will have to face it. Fortitude, the Greeks said, was the control of our reason over our aggressive instincts.

After he had thought about this, a student told me, "You know, a couple of weeks ago, I had a car accident. Someone ran into my car and rushed out of his car to accuse me of causing it. Before I had a chance to think of this question of self-control, I would have slugged him. Now, I just walked away."

There are still times, I suppose, when we should slug away. *Fortitude.* What would the world be like if there were no obstacles to overcome? Would it be a better one?

IV

We must think twice, probably, about accusing an all-good God of creating a struggle-filled world. Perhaps it is a sign of something else. A world we created for ourselves without struggle at all may be less glorious than the one we do have. Indeed, it may even be a kind of hell.

29. Tacitus said in the beginning of his *Histories*: "Never, surely, did more terrible calamities of the Roman people, or evidence more conclusive, prove that the Gods take no thought of our happiness, but only for our punishment" (I, 3).

This was written about the events of A.D. 69. Is it so strange that this could be written at the very time in which the existence of terrible calamities might very well suggest some other alternative? Is it strange that punishment and happiness are not incompatible, that it is not the gods that cause their presence in the same world?

30. My brother told me of some friends, each of whose children turned out "badly," as they say, in some way or another, really serious life problems. The parents, in fact, were rather exemplary, loyal, devoted.

"They must have done something wrong someplace," he remarked.

"Why?" I asked. "Why cannot we grant that the children choose to be the way they are? Why do we always have to blame good parents? We have to realize that children are free. They can be much, much worse than their parents. The goodness or wisdom of parents is not necessarily disproved by the childrens' vices."

31. We went to see a rather good film, *Summer Wishes, Winter Dreams*. You do not see so many movies in which both of the main characters are adults. As we left, I said, "That was a nice, rather wonderful film."

"Almost too sentimental," was the response.

"What's wrong with sentiment?" I quizzed.

Yet, we can be too sentimental, I know that. It is one of the great dangers of religion, in fact. This is why dignity, rite, and formality are important, to protect us from one another's sentiment, which cannot by nature be too public a thing, as formal worship must be.

32. It was very early on a fall morning in late October. The sun was just coming on the horizon. I took a walk outside just to feel the air, to hear the quiet against the indefinite, subdued roar of the city about to wake. The morning coolness — such things are part of our joy.

33. The Japanese Tea Garden in Golden Gate Park was empty almost, when I walked through it one day. I love the shallow, clear pools with nothing in them except newly fallen leaves floating on their surfaces. You could see the shadows of the leaves against the bottom.

A Japanese Tea Garden is a man-made thing in which all of creation exists in quietness. I have still not recovered from the beautiful gardens in Kyoto, where I was some years ago with Ev Smith, an old classmate. The shrines and temples of Shinto and Buddhist traditions seemed right in such gardens. The spirit of nature is kept about.

I had read that the Japanese Prime Minister always made a visit to a national Shinto shrine before leaving and after returning to Japan from trips abroad. When I mentioned this to a friend at dinner who had spent long years in China, he said that Shinto has in the word the notion of "The Way."

I remarked that in Tacitus, when he spoke of Christians, he called them followers of "The Way." Actually, I was probably thinking of Paul, not Tacitus, because the Felix who appeared in Tacitus was the one who recognized Paul as a Roman citizen. Paul said of him that he had "a rather accurate knowledge of 'The Way' " (*Acts*, 24: 22).

Paul said also that Felix expected a bribe, while Tacitus remarked that Felix "thought he could do any evil with impunity" (*Annals*, 12, 54). Nice character, that Felix.

My friend finally said, "Yes, we forget that Christ was an Oriental. It makes a good deal of difference if we understand what that means."

35. "I feel kind of detached today," a friend wrote.

"When shopping, I looked at all the people. They looked like they knew where they were going. Why don't I?" I have been shopping with this friend. No one would guess that here was someone wondering about directions and ways. Our inside is not always visible from our outside. This is why we must have friends.

36. I thought to myself, "Why cannot a spark of God be in all things?" What gives the living things the life that they have? The earth is beautiful. And parks are more beautiful. Good parks refashion the mysteries of wilderness and make them deeper. Creation is infinitely more strange if beauty can be made more beautiful. All parks are somehow efforts to refashion the Garden of Eden, efforts to make what is beautiful, more beautiful. The condition of mankind is that this can be done.

37. Why can the good become more good? This is a truth more disturbing to me than the vast reaches of evil.

38. To retire into ourselves — for this, I think, villas, and seashores, and mountains exist. And it is true, we can always retire into ourselves. It is essential for men and women to do this at times.

And yet, we discover so many conflicting things there. It is a sobering experience sometimes. But it is good to know our limitations and those of the world. The return to ourselves does not prove our self-sufficiency, but our self-insufficiency. And this is no little thing to realize. Indeed, it is the basis of our hope.

V

A prayer of the Athenian: "Rain, rain, O dear Zeus, down on the plowed fields of the Athenians and on the plains." In truth we ought not to pray at all, or we ought to pray in this simple and noble fashion.
– Marcus Aurelius, Meditations, V, 7.

1. "Fiat Justicia, pereat Mundus." There is no more terrible virtue than justice. We have suddenly raised a generation who have never been told this, or who have chosen not to listen. The blindness of justice is a two-edged sword. And yet, justice is good. It is a virtue.

2. Faults are freed by mercy through prayer.

3. Part of our being created equal is the realization that we are all sinners. The reason why the young cannot study politics so easily is that they do not as yet know this also includes themselves. Later, if they be honest, they know. This is why the distance between the adult and the adolescent is always and fundamentally a sort of humility.

4. "Adorn yourself with simplicity and modesty and with indifference towards the things which are neither good nor bad. Love mankind. Follow God. The poet says that law rules all. It is enough to remember that law rules all.

"As for death, whether it is a dispersion or a dissolution

41

into atoms, or annihilation, it is either extinction or change." (VII, 31, 32).

When I read and reread these lines from Marcus Aurelius, favorites of mine, to the class, the young man from Nigeria came up later and said to me, earnestly: "Thank you for reading those passages. They are very important. I had never thought of these things before."

5. During Holy Week back in 1975, I was in the orderly Italian seaport city of Bari. These were my brief meditations there:

(a) If Christianity does not best explain who I am, where am I to find a better way? Chapter 29 of *Saint Matthew* says that many will be deceived. That is not right. There are only twenty-eight Chapters in *Matthew*. It is in Chapter 24. In any case, the doctrine remains sobering to our enthusiasms, wherever it might be found.

(b) One morning out off the inner harbor about a kilometer from the railing, about ten fishing boats were out in the choppy sea. These men would soon be selling their morning catch on the warf and all over the old city of Bari in its narrow streets. Ladies were already rushing up to the fishermen already in, knowing exactly what they were looking for, how much they would pay in the bargaining. The very thought of what marvelous dishes these women could make, would soon make, caused excruciating hunger. Were it not for hunger, we should discover little of the world or the sea.

(c) Dietrich von Hildebrand said, "The Christian essentially accepts this limitation inherent in his human status." We are very concrete people, in very concrete places. People can sometimes be extremely kind to us, as were the men in Bari that I met. You cannot explain kindness. It just happens to you.

(d) The billions of stars that possibly have green planets like ours orbiting about them assure us that we are not alone in the cosmos. Yet, so far we are alone. And if we do find others, as we ought to try, will we still be alone?

(e) Thomas a'Kempis asked poignantly, "Quid dabo tibi pro omnibus istis millibus bonis?" (III, 10, 17). "What shall I give Thee for all these thousands of good things?" The answer is, of course, nothing — that is the joy and the mystery. We are not in a world in which we can pay anything back. This is one of the beliefs alternate to Christianity, that we can somehow pay back the gifts that we are. But we cannot.

(f) When you are in an obscure, far away city such as Bari on the Adriatic Sea, you realize on seeing the markets, stores, schools, cemeteries, churches, streets, houses, walks, parks, and skies, that whole lives, loves, deaths, tragedies, unbearable joys go on here all the time, events that you do not participate in. And this Bari is a city older than Marcus Aurelius himself; perhaps he visited it. But this is well, for a man or a woman cannot live more than one life. There are other lives besides our own. We must rejoice in this. There is much we miss.

(g) In Bari, I read a book about the hermits and anchorites of the fourth-century Egyptian desert, an area that still fascinates me after seeing Cairo. These monks were an odd lot, admittedly, in many cases. The author *a priori* explained that every miracle and supernatural incident related of these ancient men was due to hunger or psychological phenomenon.[5] I have learned a little about the monks of the desert from this book, but mostly I learned what Mr. Lacarrière believed he could not believe. He seemed to live in quite a small little cosmos. That is, I prefer the one we, in fact, have.

(h) Justin Kelly wrote in a journal I brought with me to Bari from Rome that, "The real antithesis to the sense of the holy is not the feeling that God is dead or absent, but the

5. Jacques Lacarrière, *Men Possessed by God* (Garden City: Doubleday, 1963).

pervasive triviality which characterizes our time." We must be careful, I think. Not only is the world large enough also for the trivial, but a good part of our time is spent in it, those mixtures of people I saw in Bari about their daily tasks, the lady who came out of her door on a narrow, curved, stone street in old Bari near the sea and the Duomo to buy some mussels or squid. She almost screamed as she bargained with the old man. I am loathe to contrast the trivial and the holy.

(i) While I was in Bari, King Faisal of Saudi Arabia was killed by his own nephew. He was probably the richest man in the world, certainly these days a most powerful one, with more oil than the rest of the world combined. The richest man in the world dies, enemies in his own household. King Faisal seemed to have been a moderate, pious Muslim man. He was in charge of Mecca and Jedda, was concerned about Jerusalem. Who are these rich, stern men? What of their Mohammed and their Allah? This religion grows more than most. It is simple, fierce. And it is also wrong to kill the richest man in the world, no less than the poorest. Prime Minister Aldo Moro was from Bari. He too was murdered.

(j) On my last morning in Bari, I bought a roll, but it was not what I wanted. I liked it, but it was not what I wanted. So I disliked it, even though I liked it. How can this be? I wondered.

6. As I get older, as I may have said, the friendships of youth and early manhood pass, or many of them do, some few remain. But they are fewer than we once had expected they would be. New friendships are made, to be sure, but it is difficult to begin with unshared times and places.

Samuel Johnson wrote:

It is a sad saying, that "most of those whom we wished to please had sunk into the grave"; and his case at forty-five was singularly unhappy, unless the circle of his friends was very narrow. I have often thought that as longevity is generally desired, and I believe, generally expected, it would be wise to be continually adding to the number of our friends, that the loss of some may be supplied by others. Friendship, "the wine of life," should, like a well-stocked cellar, be thus continually renewed; and it is a consolation to think that although we can seldom add what will equal the generous first growths of our youth, yet friendship becomes insensibly old in much less time than is commonly imagined, and not many years are required to make it very mellow, and pleasant warmth will, no doubt, make a considerable difference.

I find this comforting. And it seems mostly true to my experience also.

7. Gratitude is almost the only thing that is really ours. Yet, we cannot demand it. Indeed, its very expression is fraught with the danger that we mistake our profession of gratitude for the reality we are grateful for. Sir Joshua Reynolds once said to Samuel Johnson: "You have, however, the comfort of being relieved from your burthen of gratitude."

8. We must also be faithful to what does not yet exist. That means, roughly, that we cannot be fully content with all that is now. We persist in believing not just that there must be more, but that there also must be something better. Sometimes we call this dreaming, sometimes hope, not infrequently in our era it slips into ideology. Sometimes, it can even be a penalty, as when we fail to smell the fresh, damp sweetness of the newly cut grass on the lawn.

"See the lilies of the field, how they grow." This is the beginning of our contentment, and of our discontentment.

9. Marx wrote, "Our desires and pleasures spring from society. We measure them, therefore, by society and not by the objects which serve for their satisfaction. Because they are of a general nature, they are of a relative nature." There is much truth here. The Lord said that the poor would al-

ways be with us. And all sages have warned about greed. Both poverty and greed are relative to what our neighbors have. Our pleasures, too, mostly, though it would be false to say that nothing is good in itself or that we do not simply lack things at times.

10. The world is not a static place. Some believe that the poor are poor because the rich are rich. But the poor are poor usually because they do not know how to be rich. Everyone was once poor. The mystery is, why is not everyone so now? The answer to this latter question is usually, in modern times, because they follow the wrong idea about what causes poverty, or better, what causes wealth. The abundance of the world is relative to our intelligence and to our energies and to our sacrifices.

11. At the corner of Broadway and Lyon Street in San Francisco is an overlook. Below it is the Bay, blue, dotted with sailboats, the Palace of Fine Arts arched by its small lake in front, the masts of the boats in the Yacht Harbor, the white houses in the sun. Just seeing is a grace.

12. Several years ago, a rather odd address I gave on "The Christian Love of Animals" was published in *Vital Speeches*. A couple of months later, I received a letter from a young high school student in North Dakota, who wanted to know why I gave it. For a time, we became rather good pen-pals.

I quite liked her matter-of-factness:

I've had a half ways exciting weekend—for once. Friday—nine other kids and I went roller skating in Bismarck. We had a blast! We skated from 8:00 P.M. to 1:00 A.M. That was a lot of skating but then time goes fast when you're having fun. Saturday—was the night of the concert, and Sunday night my friend, Bonnie, and I went to Bismarck to a movie. We went to "Bad News Bears in Breaking Training." That's a funny movie! In some places, it gets serious. Such as when a father and son get back together.

Actually, we went to see "One on One," but all that was left was single seating, so we decided to go to it another time.

I do believe I'm going *crazy*! Do you want to know what I'm doing at this moment? It's 1:00 A.M. and I'm sitting here waiting for my Zuchine [sic] Bread to get done. Have you ever tasted Zuchinni [sic] Bread? It is something like Banana Bread. It is pretty good.

It was rather refreshing to learn of half "ways" exciting weekends, "going crazy," and the differing ways to spell Italian vegetables. (It is spelled zucchini; I looked it up).

13. The morning was absolutely clear and cold, a November morning. The Farallone Islands, some twenty-five miles out of the Golden Gate, were vivid against the blue ocean. I walked over to the Haight, around the base of Buena Vista Park. The city slows down on Saturday. In a coffee shop I dropped into, two men, a black man and a white man, were mutually bemoaning the President.

The black man then told of seeing an old lady being robbed on the street on the previous afternoon. The white man replied that the robberies on the #5 Fulton Street Bus, the one I usually take, are the worst in the city. But the city still remained absolutely beautiful all day. Beauty and robberies co-exist. This is our lot, though not necessarily always to our liking.

14. At the end of a review of a book castigating the United Nations, Anne Fremantle wrote: "For St. Augustine declared that any good, wherever it might be found, should be fallen upon by us as though by one starving, *sicut esuriente*, and it is a poor heart that never rejoices."

I do not want ever to forget this: *It Is a Poor Heart That Never Rejoices*.

15. My cousin called to tell me that Aunt Tess had died in Eagle Grove, in Iowa. She was a marvelous woman. For many years, whenever I was in the Midwest, I would stop by

to see her. She was always painting, talking, writing, laughing, telephoning. She never went anywhere that something fascinating and happy and enjoyable did not happen to her. Even in tragedy, which all life has, a husband killed in an automobile accident, a son recently died of cancer, she saw there was a happy side too. She really believed that the Lord giveth and the Lord taketh away. Her heart was not poor. She had found no reason why she should not also be joyful even in her eighties.

16. In late September from Neuchatel, in Switzerland, André Gide once wrote in a journal, "The history of the past is the story of all the truths that man has released. *Take upon oneself as much humanity as possible.* There is the correct formula."

But, of course, that is not the correct formula. Rather it is a prescription for a lifetime of discontent. This is one of the truths man has released in his history, that there are many very good things we shall never choose, many glorious experiences we shall never share, many deep truths we shall never know. This is why the greatest prayer is still the Great Amen, the simple "So Be It."

17. Gerard Durrell spoke one night in the Masonic Auditorium on Nob Hill in San Francisco, about his project on the Island of Jersey, quite literally in this case, his "pet" project, the Stationary Ark. Here healthy specimens of species of animals in danger of extinction are kept and cared for. He was convincing and humorous. His theme was how to care for animals, once you have captured them. His argument was that we should keep nature's beautiful beings. Once they are extinct, they cannot be replaced. He blamed man mostly for species that were lost. He neglected to be philosophic about the myriads of species that disappeared before man arrived, or species that disappeared for reasons other than human causality.

I do not mind preserving animals, if we are clear about

what we are doing, if we know our priorities. Durrell did not speak about preserving black widow spiders or malarial mosquitoes or rattlesnakes. Once we recognize that "nature" and "wilderness" no longer exist, that animals are for our use and pleasure, things will be clearer. He also neglected to talk about animals invented by man — dogs, horses, cattle, rabbits, lambs, animals crossbred to what they are not by nature, but by man. Perhaps by keeping alive species that otherwise would be extinct, we are preventing evolution. The survival of the fittest and all that sort of stuff: I wonder what ever happened to that doctrine? The abortionists seem to like it. The fittest are now those men choose to breed in zoos. The unfittest are those they kill in their own wombs.

18. We had a drink at the Top of the Fairmont Hotel, high, overlooking the illuminated, clear night, the city, the orange lights of the Bridge, Oakland on the far shore. I had forgotten that places seen again can make absences seem painful.

"You confuse nostalgia and sentiment," a friend once told me. "You misuse nostalgia, James. One cannot be 'nostalgic' about coziness, at least not unless one does not expect to experience it again, nor can one be nostalgic about something one hasn't experienced. . . ."

The pain, the returning home — but that is the point, sometimes we are nostalgic for what we have not experienced. This is why we can be nostalgic for heaven, the paradox of Christianity. Or is that wrong? Christianity does say that we are given grace, the kind that does not pass away. But that is usually the same problem. Nostalgia is somehow connected with grace, even with coziness, with home, and the pain of not yet being there.

19. Friendships sometimes interfere with the friendships of others. Yours do not always take precedence just because they are yours.

20. At Oxford, by the Thames, amid the grunts of the

crews with kerchiefs about their foreheads, my friend said, "Just once in my life I would like to do what I wanted to do." I said, "Well, of course, none of us can ever do just what we would want to do; we must always consider others." To this superpiety of mine, my friend replied, "Just once in my life, I would like to do what *I* wanted to do." This friend really did live for others.

In any case, many of the happiest moments in our lives are experienced when we are not doing just what we wanted to do. This means that happiness or salvation or whatever we want to call it comes to us not as a result of our efforts so much, but as gifts, ours to be sure, but gifts still.

21. "God's grace has need of man's apology," James K. Baxter wrote in the Thirteenth Pig Island Letter. This is so true that we hesitate to accept it. The world is full of men who think their ways of salvation are better than the Lord's. But they are wrong. Salvation is by suffering, by joy too.

22. Finally, I saw Eric Roehmer's *La Collectionneuse*, marvelous film. "La Collectionneuse" was a splendid girl by the name of Haydée, who collected boy friends she slept with. The hero of the movie was also a collector of oriental art. He tried to impose his morality on Haydée. He insisted on believing that she was merely empty, immoral.

But the girl knew she was searching for something, something she finally called a "normal relationship with someone." This is the paradox of our time, this Haydée, that we can do anything we want; but if we do, we cannot usually have what we want — that is, a normal relationship with somebody.

23. The student behind the desk in Gleeson Library was in one of my classes. "Beautiful day," he said to me. And it was, cold, clear. "Yes," I answered, "but there is a fog sitting out there in the Ocean, which will come in soon." "I hope not," he remarked, "I prefer sunny days."

But I don't prefer them, though I like them too. I prefer the fog and the rain. However, I decided not to tell him. Fog and rain have to be loved mysteriously, not everyone is given their secrets.

24. A windy, rainy, November night in San Francisco. I had been anxious to hear the concert at the Veterans' Auditorium, an all Bach Concert — a suite, three Brandenburg Concerti, the Sixth, Third, and Second, each glorious.

The first movement of the Sixth was very deep, memorable. Of course, the Third and the Second are beyond compare. I have not forgotten Plato and Aristotle, who hint that music is to be our leisure, if not also our paradise. We take the "heavenly choirs" today as a sort of analogy, at best. But in fact they may just be the reality. I hope so, especially if in paradise, I learn to play these marvelous Bach concerti. I shall not do so in this life, of course, and this is sad, somehow, to me.

25. The trumpet of the Second Brandenburg Concerto is powerful and delicate. The audience responded very enthusiastically to Karl Richter's conducting. These concerti were first played for Christian Ludwig, Margraf of Brandenburg, on March 24, 1721.

Beautiful things never end. Music perhaps is the only art that cannot pass away because men will always be there to play it again, as if the Margraf Christian Ludwig were still about.

26. The great modern sin, they say, is to act differently from what you profess. It does not matter much what you profess, but do not act otherwise. Nevertheless, it is easy to ignore the fact that hypocricy is a virtue when our profession is nonsense. There is no way to escape abstract justice or check on our own profession of virtue unless there is something greater than justice. And justice is very great.

27. There are those who are angry at God because only justice is not in this world. In a truly just world, the last would be the last, as they should be. But the main message we receive from beyond the stars, or wherever, confounds all of this. There are men who would be first were the world

created in justice. They resent a God who overturns their rightful place in the universe.

28. The world is filled with splendid things. Count them.

29. Most of the truly great things that men have ever done go unrecorded. We should not delude ourselves that the storehouse of goodness is exhausted by what little we know.

30. The most extraordinary thing about the universe is not the evil in it. Rather it is that God will have mercy on whom he will have mercy. Harlots and publicans somehow enter the Kingdom first. And this is absolutely unjust. We should not deceive ourselves about this.

31. At the beginning of *La Collectionneuse*, there is a sort of prologue that discusses the relation between love and ugliness. Can we love someone who is ugly? Do we love because of beauty, even one beautiful thing, or does what we first love become beautiful to us? And do beauty and ugliness make any difference? Can the beautiful be bad? The ugly good? Yet, beauty is wrenching of itself. It can break down our world. Perhaps that is why there is so much of it about. We have so much that needs breaking down.

32. I read some *Deuteronomy* — "the steadfast love" — perhaps the greatest, most consoling phrase in the Old Testament. This is better than justice, for we are not always just. Yet, we want our friends to be steadfast throughout our injustices, in spite of them. Loyalty, too, is a part of what is not just justice.

33. I asked the class, for no special reason except that the topic was somehow on geopolitics, "Why is Cincinnati, Ohio, a seaport?" A dear young girl responded, quizzically, "Because there are boats there?"

It really made it a better day, even if it was not exactly the answer I had in mind.

34. I wrote an essay on an NBI word processor in which I mentioned that such machines make their products flaw-

less, what with wordstar and such. The editor of the journal (*Spiritual Life*) wrote back: "May I suggest (with gentle humor) that your word processor corrects spelling but not typographical errors (e.g., kindergar*d*en, cotem*i*nous, bul*l*its, fascin*t*ates)? Or perhaps you want these left in as is?"

Two of the errors of this "flawless" piece, the no "r" in cote*r*minous and the extra "t" in fascinates, were due to lack of my proofreading. The other two, kindergarten and bullet, I suspect, I have always misspelled. There is something consoling, I suppose, to be corrected of a lifetime of spelling errors, unnoticed by a not so flawless writer.

35. The inside roof light of the car would not turn off as it is supposed to do when you shut the door of the car. I tried slamming the door. Then, I looked for a switch on the light. Next, I tried the switch which is supposed to cut the lights off when the door is shut. At last, in exasperation, I took off the plastic, transparent cover and managed to turn the light bulb enough to disconnect it.

Next day, I went to the garage to have it repaired. The mechanic, Jerry Timmins, snapped the bulb back in, put the plastic cover back on, then calmly turned off the overhead light switch near the steering column.

He was kind enough to make no comment on my mechanical abilities.

36. For fifty cents, I bought a 1929 Literary Digest *World Atlas* and a copy of Rousseau's *Emile*, over on Clement Street. The *Atlas*, of course, is out-of-date, but then an old Atlas is often better than nothing. Continents do not change much. Besides I often have occasion to know how the world was divided in 1929, the year after I was born.

Emile begins with the famous sentence, "Everything is good as it comes from the hands of the author of nature; but everything degenerates in the hands of man." I wonder if it is quite so simple. The only alternatives are not between good and degeneration. And yet, in a way, Rousseau was saying no more than Scripture, except that he did not suggest that the author of nature is capable of restoring what the hands of man touch, but in his own way.

37. A letter from traveling friends:

> We were in North and Central Wales, stayed at three different hotels which the children loved. First night, we stayed at Rayadear, second in Corwen, and the third on Snowdonia, the last the greatest. We were very high in the mountains. The days were crystal clear and the leaves were all golden; the air was so clear you could walk for miles, and we did, never tired. I saw the sun set and rise. I'll never forget those incredible sights. Christ, I'm such a romantic — when I am in such situations, I want everyone to feel the beauty as I do. The children are a bit young to appreciate such vastness. So I did it on my own, so to speak. I took many walks alone and enjoyed the peace of it all.

There is always this tension, I think, between beauty and aloneness, between peace and wanting everyone else to enjoy it all. Beauty must be experienced before it is expressed. But once we behold it, it is maddening not to share it with others.

38. Walking down Clement Street in San Francisco on a warm, but wet afternoon, rather crowded, about four, I passed a young couple, in long baggy clothing. As I walked by, the girl said to the boy in a loud, quite angry, yet poignant voice: "Yes, but I *want* to have the baby. . . ."

I hurried along faster, so I could not hear any more. I began to feel rather sick. "Sane woman, dumb bastard," I thought to myself.

39. Self-deception is real enough. We really do want the world to turn out right, to love everybody, to help everybody, to enlighten everybody. Yet, we are full of cross purposes,

even within ourselves. We want so many things in a world where we only have an allotted time that allows for a few. This is really why we have the Commandments, I think, so that we have a chance, at least, of fully appreciating what few things we do have time for, the best ones.

40. "You write, 'It's the time you waste with your friends that counts (*Little Prince*).' I think that the time with friends is *never* wasted!" I stand corrected in this. Time with friends is never wasted. Aristotle, I think, even suggests that this is what life is about, something in its own way the New Testament confirms in a manner not even Aristotle could have imagined.

41. The mystery is not that our desires are so universal and all-consuming, although by this, we know we are alive and are being driven by something beyond us. Nor is it just that we have so little time, even if we are allotted the full span of four score years.

The mystery is rather that some things *do* satisfy us. And because of this, we begin to suspect that there is a real connection between ourselves and the world, neither of which we made, that there is a satisfaction for what is infinite in us.

42. We are a nation that now believes that our leaders should be just, even if we are not. We are a nation that believes that there is no dogmatic proof that can be taught in our universities establishing the certitude of justice. We are a nation which gets angry at a Solzhenitsyn for telling this about ourselves. Yet, we are all angry when we are treated unjustly, even though our reason says that we are not the best judges in our own cases. This must mean, in a way, that we never think justice is done to us. I hope so, because if it is in any absolute sense, we are doomed. Our hope lies in what is not justice.

43. The National Association of Broadcasters Code Authority banned Santa Claus from use in toy commercials

on television because Santa is considered to be an authority figure and a product of fantasy.[6]

I was at my sister's when I read this. It practically ruined Christmas for me. It is simply unjust — even I use that word — to deprive children of fantasy figures, not to mention symbols of authority.

44. There is hope in justice, but no ultimate hope.

45. Charles Boyer was over ninety years old, a wonderful old French priest I knew many years in Rome, before his death. He was a fine scholar, whose books I had read years before meeting him. He wrote once in *L'Osservatore Romano*, that God revealed Christ's divinity, but he was not able to force us to believe in it. "And he has not made us see it because only in the next life is Christ's divine glory seen."

Perhaps it is unjust of God to force an old man to wait so long. Then again, perhaps justice does not define God so well. In a sense, the longer we wait, the more we expect. This may be why old age is a gift, not a burden.

46. To pray in a simple fashion is a confidence. We know the cosmos possesses an incredible complexity. We know too that the infinite cross-purposes and confusions of mankind leave us always on the verge of depression.

Still, there is no value in pretense. We are confident that we are not alone. Rain falls on the plowed fields of Iowa, where my cousin Vincent still farms and on the plains, on the just and the unjust.

6. *Arizona Republic*, December 24, 1974.

VI

Keep yourself simple, good, pure, serious, free from affectation, a friend of justice, a worshipper of the gods, kind, affectionate, strenuous in all right acts. Strive to advance toward what philosophy has made you. Reverence the gods and help man. Life is short. There is only the fruit of this earthly life, a pious disposition and social acts.
— *Marcus Aurelius, Meditations, VI, 30.*

1. I voted in a local election one day in San Francisco. I really had little feeling one way or another for most of the candidates, less for the endless propositions and declarations of policy, except for the one that wanted me to declare myself for universal day-care centers. This was Rousseau again. They would not work in San Francisco, in any case. Many think the family is the origin of evil. Joseph Sobran, in his *Single Issues*, is right when he suggests that what is being proposed is the reduction of everyone to the care of the state.[7]

2. My friend, Jim Latham, spent many years in Paris. He said that the Paris Opera has a rule that, when the

7. Joseph Sobran, *Single Issues* (New York: Human Life Press, 1983).

language is anything but French, the cast receives four times as much pay. This is why you never get anything there except in French. The saying goes, he said, with a twinkle, "For when you already have perfection, why strive for anything else?"

3. When you touch someone's heart, it is said, you are no longer the same. And it is a bit frightening. John McKenzie said in the *Jerome Bible Commentary* that the Hebrews said that we think with our hearts, not with our minds. And there is this about the Old Testament, a tremendous sense of authenticity and depth that is only analogous to our experience in which we reach the depth of another, with all that responsibility and awe that comes from the realization that there really is another to be touched.

4. Dr. Johnson responded to Oliver Goldsmith: "No man is obliged to do as much as he can do. A man is to have a part of his life to himself." There is a certain pride in the feeling that we ourselves must do everything. Privacy is the condition of our being able to be in public. Johnson's point was that someday, we must retire. And most do so with a good heart. The point is also that during each day, we must have a bit of time for retirement, what the monks and Marcus Aurelius, Emperor, used to call meditation.

5. What happens when we suddenly discover that more exists to the world than we had thought, when we see a beauty or a tragedy that overturns our limits, when we meet someone who convulses our very being in a way we simply did not know possible? We are caught between following a star and remembering the now common things that were once also overpowering, new, and dramatic. The law is to make us free, free to follow the star, equally free not to. The fact that the world is so much richer than we ever expected is not itself the great law. The great law is rather that all is to be sacrificed for a friend, the whole world, sometimes.

6. In one of my classes in Rome, a Vietnamese student gave a report on Tito and Djilas. Afterward, he said, "You see, I had a difficult time, as I did not know anything about

them before, so it was not a good report." I replied, "That is why I gave the assignment to you. Now you know something about these men. Good reports about something you already know are pretty useless."

7. It was raining when I left the science center. I walked quite quickly back to the main building. The air was fresh in San Francisco. I was wet. But I felt good; the rain does fall on the just and the unjust. It was doing so now. I like that part of God's plan, especially when I am unjust.

8. We should try to see things through another's eyes. But this is a criterion for sympathy and understanding, not one of reality. If we literally see things through another's eyes, we only see the images of another, a kind of reality, to be sure, but not the thing itself from which our gaze must begin. If we all see only the same things, through one of our friend's eyes, we shall miss the billions of visions all about us, especially our own. We are not all meant to see exactly the same things. This is why we all have eyes. It is also why we all have endless topics of conversation when with one another.

The search for perfection can be a terrible thing, in individuals or in society. We are to be perfect as our heavenly Father is perfect. We are told that the Lord prefers mercy to sacrifice. Yet, he whom we should fear most is the one who insists upon the perfection of others first. If you want to test any man or movement on this score, see if it can accept this as its initial starting point: "We are all first sinners."

10. Professor Leo Strauss said, "Affluence does not cause the deepest evils. . . . Every human being is what he is by the fact that he looks up to something." The deepest things are spiritual. What we look up to; what we look down upon. "Whoever heard of a man making himself a tyrant in order to keep warm?" so Aristotle put it in *The Politics*.

11. Remember this about life: A lot of rules have a lot of exceptions.

12 Should we live with those we cannot get along with? Those who are downright bastards? Does faith tell us to

accept the situation or to improve it? Or does it tell us to suffer? Can suffering ever be creative? Is it possible to avoid, not just physical suffering, but the kind of anguish that comes with our not getting our own way? When you confront something that is wrong, you do not have to refashion your philosophy to call it right. You have to acknowledge first that it is wrong. Then you may have to suffer it. Or change it.

Lovely and dear people have sometimes screwy ideas. Not always, not necessarily, but sometimes. They are still lovely and dear people. Their ideas are still screwy.

13. John's uncle was a past-President of the American Heart or Cancer Association. I forget which, the one that is against smoking. Helen was showing her uncle and aunt through Venice. They rented a gondola. The young gondolier, as they pushed off, lit a cigarette.

For the benefit of her husband's uncle, Helen felt she should explain, a bit in jest, to the young man that smoking was a danger to his health, might even cause cancer and early death. This in Italian. The gondolier kept on shoving the bark into the canal and smoking. Finally, he glanced down and sighed, "Ah, Signora, siamo tutti qui in passaggio." — "Ah, Madame, we are all here only in passage."

Everyone was delighted with this response, including the uncle. So we take our chances. Sooner or later, life's end is ours too. A few years, here and there, do they matter so much? Perhaps they do to those who do not believe in forever.

Later, years later, as I thought of this incident, I thought that most of the antinuclear war people seem to hold that there is no forever, that keeping alive for as long as possible is the only meaning to life.

15. Ancient Christian culture was universal. It demanded that all men belonged, neither gentile nor Greek were excluded. But today, we maintain that we all belong to

different cultures. We are each different. All we have to do is follow our own culture.

"Let's suppose," I announced to a student in class one day, "you are a Hindu lady in the last century, so when your husband died, you are supposed to leap joyfully on his funeral pyre as your culture and your religion insisted, even though the reason the Hindu had this custom was, apparently, to keep wives from poisoning their husbands and making off with the loot."

She looked at me, puzzled. I went on: "Now, let's suppose you, as the Hindu lady, are also very well read in Aristotle, Locke, and Rousseau, and the British Raj tells you the reason you should not jump on the pyre is because that's not what good widows do in Salisbury or Lyon or Freiburg. And supposing there is no universal culture as the ancients thought, but only differing cultures, each with its own folkways, as modern thought maintains. How would you answer logically the British Raj, who commanded you not to jump on the pyre in the name of his reason?"

"I'd jump into the pyre," she answered with a frown.

"Correct," I said.

16. In class, I was assigning some readings from the New Testament concerning political thought in Christianity. While writing on the blackboard that the students should read the Thirteenth Chapter of the *Epistle to the Romans*, I asked a student: "Who wrote the *Epistle to the Romans?*"

"I never heard of the *Epistle to the Romans*," he replied earnestly.

Astonished, I repeated, "You never heard of the *Epistle to the Romans?*"

"No," he insisted.

The previous year, I had asked a class of thirty how many had ever heard of Homer. Three put up their hands.

17. The New Testament, along with the Psalms, is the most read book in the history of man. What does it mean to one's own humanity to have gone all the way through one's formal education without ever having read these sources or having been required to read them? It is worth some meditation, this lacuna. What will the world be like when it has forgotten the New Testament? Fellini, I believe, asked this question when he redid Petronius' *Satyricon*. Not very nice, it seems, but rather like we find in the press oftentimes, about what we do every day.

18. The translators of the King James Version of Scripture wrote: "Truly (good Christian reader), we never thought from the beginning that we should make a new translation, nor yet to make a bad one a good one . . . but to make a good one better."

Sometimes, we get uncanny visions of the good and the evil so it is not often we are reminded so clearly that a good world is still full of life and activity and delight. At times, it seems that evil is in the world to prevent it from being dull. We forget that such is rather why good is in the world. Evil probably is just that, ultimately, dull.

19. There is no question that the control of our desires is a part of happiness, as Stoics, like Marcus Aurelius, taught. There are, thus, two ways to get what we want: one is to change the world, the other is to change ourselves. But controlling the world by mastering our desires can be a form of human pride. But so can changing the world.

20. Would you abolish sadness if you could?

21. John Cage wrote in *A Year from Monday*: "Asked a Spanish doctor what she thought about the human mind in a world of computers. She said computers are always right but life isn't about being right."

It isn't about being wrong, either. Rather, it is about being right sometimes, wrong at other times, about being able to laugh at even our sins.

22. I drank a very cold orange juice, which I squeezed

myself. We should like what is to be liked. We forget that to our pleasures there is also added a kind of implicit challenge about how we accept the world, a sort of sly mocking of our solemnities.

Why should there be, then, anything at all which really pleases us and gives us pleasure? Why are there things that not merely keep us alive but satisfy us, make us really say, "That *was* good!" The point here is not that "the best things in life are free" — which they may not be — but rather that what gives us pleasure, the very faculties and actions in which we experience it most intensely, are already there, for our enjoyment. We are to grow oranges, and squeezed orange juice is good. We already have such a capacity; no one invented it for us, though we did invent the squeezer.

23. After several days of rain, it cleared. The Farallones were easily seen miles off Ocean Beach. I made a sandwich, of San Francisco's delicious sourdough French bread, some ham, cheese, and mustard. I climbed the bus to the beach.

I was sitting eating the sandwich, watching some surfers at the end of the beach near the Cliff House. Everything was very clear. Some dogs were playing in the sand. A very tiny little girl, hardly two years old, dressed in a white sweater, dark dotted pants, a half-fallen ponytail, came walking a bit unsteadily toward the rocks at the end of the beach.

Her mother was a couple of hundred yards back talking to a crippled old man on the beach. A Chinese boy came down the far steps to do some push-ups. Another young man was just below me, drinking a beer, eating his lunch. You are encouraged when you know there are people who just like to watch the waves.

The little girl, meanwhile, was clapping her hands, eying the dogs. She wanted to pet them but was a bit afraid. Everyone could see that if she walked straight ahead, she would be trapped by the waves. Yet, too, you knew that the little girl was actually perfectly safe. I was watching her;

the young man below was watching her; the Chinese boy had his eye on her — a little girl, on the beach sort of alone, enjoying the water, the dogs, glancing at the Chinese boy. Such a little girl is an absolute. The whole world is designed to protect her.

24. There are two magnificent windmill structures at the ocean end of Golden Gate Park. One, now completely restored, is surrounded by Queen Wilhelmina's Tulip Garden. These mills used to pump water into the park, I believe. The other one is being restored. This is what a city is for, I think, to keep the past by making it beautiful, interesting, quaint, a place to go at the end of the Park.

25. If you turn down a certain path, you meet only those on the same road.

26. A young boy about seventeen or so, came jogging by me about Nineteenth Avenue. His head was thrown back, his hair flowing. He had a smile on his face, as though he was really exhilarated. There were myriads of blue autumn flowers on the path, many red fall berries.

27. About Sixth Avenue, I thought I saw my cousin Linda zipping around Kennedy Drive on a ten-speed bicycle. She was wearing long red stockings and a blue jumper, watching for the traffic, but I did not attract her attention before I realized it was she. A couple of days later, I told her about seeing her in the Park. She said that she does not own a ten-speed bike and was at work at the time. Sometimes you are glad you didn't shout.

About Third Avenue, two trim Jewish matrons with racquets were walking briskly along. One was saying in a loud, accented voice: "No. I do not go to group, I stick to analysis. It suits my personality better."

At Stanyan Street, the school buses were just discharging their quotas of happily bused children in the right proportions, according to the law of the land. There was a very cute black girl, two Chinese children, three whites. They were really dear and seemed to get along well.

28. Few people greet each other on streets and in parks

in America, or at least not in large cities. Europe seems more friendly, perhaps because it is safer, though there are codes there about when one greets and when one does not. This is, of course, the great American project, simply to make the country safe, not for democracy, but just for walking and strolling in its parks and streets.

29. "Love God and do what you will." That is St. Augustine. If you love one another, the one thing you cannot do is what you will.

30. "This book is for you to read when you next feel like a novel — you may like it — I just really wanted to give you something." Now, I forget the novel given. Yet, I do not forget the wanting to give. The best gifts are the givers.

31. "Another Galbraith quip — Wednesday night prayer meeting at the Presbyterian Church (somewhere in Minnesota) for the 'peculiarly pessimistic.'

32. "Why the sudden interest in food and drink and recipes for same? Are you writing on the subject? (I should send you Sophia Loren's new cookbook—.)"

I cannot help thinking of how the late Groucho Marx would have responded to such a setup like that—"Forget the cookbook, just send Sophia Loren!" I always loved Groucho Marx, even more his brothers.

33. Sometimes, there are no possibilities. What was it the logic book used to say? *Ex non posse sequitur nihil?* Or *ex non posse sequitur non esse?* or something. What is not possible cannot happen. However, the fact remains. Sometimes, there are no possibilities.

34. In the *Little Flowers of Saint Francis*, there is a marvelous story about Brother Giles who went to visit St. James of Campostella. As he returned from this very strenuous, ascetic trip of fasting and alms-giving, this story is recorded:

> And as he returned through Lombardy, a man called to him, to whom he went readily enough, thinking to receive an alms from him; but as he

stretched out his hand, the other placed in it a couple
of dice, inviting him to play. And Brother Giles, re-
plying humbly said, "God forgive thee, son," and went
on his way. And thus he went through the world,
receiving such contempt and taking it all peacefully.

To accept contempt peacefully is a very difficult kind of virtue for us to accept, let alone practice. Nevertheless, such a
practice, I suspect, is more efficacious than we admit. But it
is hard to associate spirituality with not throwing the dice.

What would have been the lesson for spiritual history
had good Brother Giles shot craps, and won? I think the
point would have remained about the same, probably that
God favors the humble, even. Like the lot falling on Matth-
ias, in *Acts*.

35. William Lanoutte concluded his article about the
rapid progress of the American wine industry this way:
" 'The first rule is that there are no rules,' Julius Wilie says.
'Let your palate be your guide. Serve whatever wine you
like, whenever you choose to serve it.' Moreover, Wilie
added, 'Don't take wine too seriously. Let's face it, if someone has paid $50 for a bottle of wine, he'll have a hard time
enjoying it. It sort of spoils it for him to drink it, and if he
keeps it around and just admires it, that wastes it too.'

"Drinking wine shouldn't be a solemn occasion. It
should be fun."[8]

But wine is for solemn occasions too.

36. I cannot decide sometimes whether the less one
knows about what one misses is better or worse.

37. J. R. R. Tolkien died on September 5, 1973, in Bour-
nemouth, England.

In the *Return of the King*, it said: " 'Since they falter no
longer, it seems, may I now spend my life as I will?'

'Few may do so with honor,' he answered."

A life with honor is usually not composed entirely of

8. *National Observer,* November 10, 1973.

doing what we would. And even when it is, the honor derives from choosing what we ought, our particular destiny.

38. Mel Brooks said, "Immortality is a by-product of good work. Masterpieces are not for artists, they're for critics. Critics can't even make music by rubbing their back legs together. My message to the world is, 'Let's swing, sing, shout, make noise! Let's not mimic death before our time comes! Let's be wet and noisy!' "

To be immortal, we first have to be mortal, that is, alive, wet, and noisy.

39. "But Marcus (Aurelius), who, had he known Christianity better, must have found much to admire in it, can find no word of praise for the blind, stupid courage of the Christian (martyred in Lyon during his reign)." This is Harold Mattingly in his *Roman Imperial Civilization*.

40. "The article is right about real women not being impressed by power, money, or fancy cars. They are impressed by goodness, gentleness, and strength. That is for sure."

41. This Roman Emperor, Marcus Aurelius, said that we should reverence the gods and help men. This was not the only time something like this was said in the ancient world. But it cannot be repeated often enough, especially by Emperors. It is not always easy for good men to understand other good men, though real women may have an easier time of it.

Christianity seems, sometimes, to suggest that it is the best of men who have the most difficulty with the God who came to be among us. The parade of those who are to enter the Kingdom first does not seem to be led by what we would call good men, or even good women. It is led by harlots and publicans, in fact.

VII

Love only that which happens to you and is woven into your destiny. For what is more suited to your needs?
– Marcus Aurelius, Meditations, VII, 57.

1. I saw Truffaut's *Night for Day*. It had been a stormy November day, clouds lifted briefly before sunset to make the most glorious sight on the Sundown Sea. Then it began to rain again. These are perfect days for me. And though I love the rain, I do not walk enough in it. The movie, to return to it, was about a movie being made, a tragedy. The people in the movie become the real actors of their destiny, which they must themselves carry out.

2. History is not a drama, but there is drama in history, comedy, tragedy, and adventure, too.

3. At the end of *The Republic*, Plato recounts a myth about our destiny. In the story, we are all given a chance to choose our lot in a second creation. We all choose the lot we had in our first creation, or we do not improve much, in any case. Plato suggested that we ought to be sure to choose correctly the first time.

4. Evolution is very deceiving. It gives the impression that we are somehow nearer a goal because we live in our

century rather than the century or two before us. This is not
obviously so. We have little advantage over the ancients. All
progress is ambiguous. The rule is this: Where evil abounds,
grace abounds more fully. This is the only sense in which we
are created equal.

5. A young man said he did not want to study religion
because it did not solve the personal problems he was interested in. My friend said to him: "But you do not study
physics to solve the problems you are interested in. You
study physics to discover what it thinks and says about itself. Only when you know this can you decide."

The criterion of religion is not that of solving personal
problems, but of explaining to us what the world and ourselves are, such that we can change our lives, if needs be.
That one of the basic notions of the New Testament is
"metanoia" — repent, change — is no accident. Religion
does not conform to us, but we to it. Otherwise, we are locked
totally into ourselves and our own desires.

Elizabeth Anscombe, the English philosopher, said
something similar:

> The teaching which I have rehearsed is indeed
> against the grain of the world, against the current of
> our time. But that, after all, is what the Church as
> teacher is for. The truths that are acceptable to a
> time — as, that we owe it as a debt of justice to
> provide out of our superfluity for the destitute and
> the starving — these will be proclaimed not only by
> the Church: The Church teaches *also* those truths
> that are hateful to the spirit of an age.

These are powerful words, and we know not what problems need to be solved, unless we be taught, against the
spirit of our age.

6. Jack Newfield said, "it is one of the depressing char-
acteristics of America that an idea can travel from the un-
derground to 'show biz' popularity to nostalgia in six

months." Another characteristic is that many of the world's greatest and profoundest ideas are never even heard because of this immense traffic of things passing from here to nostalgia and back in six months. This is why we are told to reflect, in ourselves, against the spirit of an age.

7. There are two mysteries about those who suffer in silence. The one is the effect on the one who causes unjust suffering; the other is on the destiny of the one suffering. There is much suffering that cannot be attributed to someone else's injustice or fault. We have no way of not facing up to this fact at least sometimes in our lives, of either deciding that there is no god or that he is the cause of our suffering. If there is a true religion, it strikes me, it will be one that begins and ends about this fact.

8. We all want to be loved, Truffaut said, actors more than others. The handshake was invented as a sign of friendship, but this is not enough for actors. This is why they kiss one another more.

This may perhaps be true, but it may also be nearer to the opposite. The mystery of love is still mystery, even when it is public. But if it never is private, it will destroy itself. What was it a friend said about exclusivity?

> Exclusivity can make the difference between close friendship and simple friendship or acquaintance. When I was a teen-ager, I was one of a group of fifteen girls who were all supposed to be equally good friends. You can imagine that trying to be close friends with fifteen people simultaneously, if nothing more, was exhausting and left no time for anything else. But probably more important than exhaustion, one cannot possibly give of himself equally to all. Subsequently, I have never managed more than one good friend at a time.

When there is a sense of proportion and acceptance, then can what is exclusive finally become in a way public. Friendships require privacy. Yet, they are the strongest thing in the world. Aristotle said that the absolute tyrant, to be successful, must not allow them.

9. The last time I was in Milan, we went to an evening Mass in the great Gothic Duomo, at that time all covered with repair scaffolding. The dark, beautiful interior, also half in repair, was a place so many families came to with their children to hear early evening Mass.

William Murray wrote: "The Duomo was officially declared completed in 1950, but the proclamation was purely symbolic, for one section after another is constantly undergoing repair. In Milanese dialect, the phrase, 'la fabbrica del Domm' (building the Duomo) means a job that will never be finished."

I hope this is true. It is the perfect symbol of our loves and our joys, things that constantly need working on, things that when completed, yet take care and concern, things that are so beautiful that we never stop being astonished by them.

10. We started with a consideration of Augustine. To the class, I remarked: "I shall begin by saying that last year I visited the Church — San Pietro in Ciel d'Oro, marvelous name, Saint Peter's in the Sky of Gold — in Pavia where Augustine's bones now are preserved. And how did Augustine's bones finally make it from Africa to Pavia? The Saracens, of course."

Just to recall his name, Augustine, reminds us of that "restlessness" in which we are all made. No matter how much we are content in our joys and our loves, there still rise the bones of Augustine to recall to us that the city we are seeking is not ours.

11. What happens when we insist on believing that men are motivated only by virtuous or altruistic motives? We must find some reason why things do not work out as they should, were humans actually all so good. We must find a scapegoat in evil men or things. We need not believe all

motives are selfish or distorted, but we must recognize that some can be and are. If we believe that all men are sinners, we cannot insist that nothing ever goes wrong. And if things do go wrong, as they do, we still must live in the world. Is there a faith that can live in such a world?

12. The concept of home is the profoundest metaphysical problem of them all.

13. "It is a brilliant fall day, the kind that makes you ache somewhere deeply inside. I have spent much of the night and morning day-dreaming. . . ." But opposite moods come to me on a brisk, windy rainy day in San Francisco, when I could not but wander about in the wetness and moisture that are so much a part of this air. My friend was right, though. We do ache on beautiful days. Is it because of the days themselves, or because brilliant fall days, or rainy brisk days, are part of what we remember? The very fact that we can ache deeply inside at all means that we are not complete. When we know this one thing, we have begun to touch the deepest mystery about ourselves.

14. Augustine said: "Ah, Christians, heavenly shoot, ye strangers on earth, who seek a city in heaven, who long to be associated with the holy angels, understand that ye have come here on this condition only, that ye should soon depart. Ye are passing on through the world, endeavoring to reach Him who created it."

However much we might like to ignore this, and most of the universities in the world do ignore it, Augustine described very well both our feeling about ourselves in this world — we are strangers — and the Christian reason for it — we shall soon depart to reach Him who created us all. I believe it is a good practice to memorize these lines and to repeat them to ourselves any time we hear a new theory explaining diversely who we are and where we are going.

15. At South Lake Tahoe, the slot machines were very busy at Midnight. Ordinary people were winning or losing various small sums, usually the latter. We do have a gam-

bling instinct, a challenge to the very fates, perhaps, the belief that somehow the deities will be kind to us. Outside the casinos, it was snowing heavily, beautiful, fresh snow in the mountains at night, as we returned to my brother's.

16. Discouragement is not easily accounted for. Courage is more straight-forward. We need praise and success at the same time, and we need friends. Yet, neither friends or praise are objects of command or payment of debt. They come when we least expect them.

In the meantime, there is loneliness. Without some sense of discouragement and loneliness, there is no spiritual depth in us usually. I wonder if this is why we were not born into a paradise? At least, it is a fact, we weren't. For some reason, undoubtedly divine, we were not begotten into perfection.

17. There were three giant slot machines at Harrah's at Tahoe, probably more now. A very old man was playing the fifty cent machine for at least an hour while I watched him. He spent a fair amount of his own money. He looked discouraged.

Suddenly, a pretty young woman walked by, took out a silver dollar, walked on up to the giant dollar machine, and immediately hit a jackpot for $150. She shrieked happily and was surrounded by her husband and delighted friends. The old man just went on playing the fifty cent machine.

18. Cardinal McKeffery of New Zealand died. He was a very tall, white-haired old man, erect, honorable. I chatted with him the July I was in Wellington. We were in his study, a very old, quaint sort of a room, which he preferred to anything more ornate. He was the one who made it possible for me to visit New Zealand. After he died, I wondered if I ever thanked him.

19. These are some brief reminders of New Zealand for me. I began jotting them down, sketchy, on a low flight from Dunedin to Christchurch on the South Island, a clear, cold winter day, in July, such an odd time for winter for me. The

sun made dark, striking shadows of the trees and sheep and fences on the green of this fertile place. I recall especially the white frost at Mosgiel, a place named somehow by a relative of Robert Burns, the Scottish poet, the name of the Burns family home. This itself is important, that we name places because we want to remember, to commemorate, from far away.

20. There are comparatively few sounds in New Zealand, though, as John Cage said in *Silence*, there are sounds everywhere if we will but listen — sounds of wind, waves, work, birds, chatter. There were cars sometimes, and cows were in the green winter pastures. Meantime, there was the beautiful black and red and brown of New Zealand alongside the white sheep and green of winter.

21. On a Saturday afternoon in Dunedin, I was invited to a rugby game. In the stadium, men relaxed. There was a piper band from Green Island, the opposing team. Here, almost at the end of the world, men attended the game, were taken out of themselves, the eternal wonder of who will win and who will lose.

22. Dunedin has a hillside cemetery that overlooks the long finger of its inner bay, which almost reaches back to the sea through its hilly streets. Dunedin — Edinburgh — the town of Eden. Scotland was everywhere, yet so far away. Did the stern ancestors of the last century come here to establish again the Kingdom? They founded in fact a quiet town that ceases weekday activity on Friday night. South of their lovely home, there is only the vast, cold of Anartica and its surrounding oceans.

23. Back in San Francisco, in the late fall, I found a book of Mauriac, the French novelist, with a letter of Gide: "It is precisely your restlessness that is the most Christian element in you." This is right, of course. There are things we do not know we want. Not to know this is the penalty of doubt and unbelief.

24. The most important capacity we have is the capacity

to be surprised. It means that the world that we are to be given is so much greater than the world we choose to live in. But this further surprise can only happen if we understand that the world we live in is itself already an infinite surprise.

25. "I do not see how Augustine can say that a Christian may have to punish someone, yet he cannot hate him in the process," a sincere student asked me in class one morning.

"If you walked past a little child being beaten by someone," I answered, "you could not help but hating the deed. You would not be a man if you did not try to stop it. Yet, you must understand and forgive, even while you fight and hate the harm to the child."

26. At about Twentieth Avenue and Geary in San Francisco, there is a good doughnut and coffee shop. I had been walking for a long time. It was cold and fresh. I was tired. I walked in and asked the elderly lady for a doughnut and drank the warm coffee, watched the other customers come in and go out. I felt much better walking the rest of the way home.

I am pleased that such things exist in the world. But such contentment is paradoxical too. The very fact of satisfaction is itself an affirmation that the universe and I are not totally disproportionate. And yet, there is no reason we should expect this unless somehow the world is meant to be a gift to us.

27. "Right now, I am worried about mother. She seems to be putting her affairs in order, sending bronzed baby shoes (mine) and old letters and generally sorting things out. Her letters are rather sad. I do not know whether she doesn't feel well—she doesn't say—or just feels she is aging faster. (I know the feeling!!)"

I remember an old American priest who died in Rome a couple of years ago. He knew he had little time left. I went to see him one night. He only had one book left, a Bible or breviary perhaps. He had already sorted everything out.

He died a few days later. Strange, I could not think of any way to talk to him. He was cheerful enough, but he had lost interest in the only world we immediately had in common. Yet, I knew he was right. My friend's mother too is merely beginning to tell us what the old Cephalus told Socrates at the beginning of *The Republic*, what it is like along the road we all must eventually travel.

28. "We must keep open to change," a friend said. "We get too easily set in our ways; we do not know what is happening." I am, however, rather more interested in things that do not change so much. I am aware that preservation is also adaptation, the old Burkean principle. Still, I cannot help but feeling that advocates, apologists, enthusiasts for change risk a certain shallowness.

29. The existence of laughter is a most curious aspect of creation. Yet, there is laughter that mocks and is bitter. Both kinds of laughter unexpectedly transform both good and evil into something profounder than we might otherwise suspect. Laughter is mainly something heard. The ear may really be capable of hearing the sounds of eternity.

30. When my brother, now in Reno, had a place at Lake Tahoe, I recall a winter morning. The sun made a brilliant contrast of white, blue on the water, and dark green under the snow-laden trees. We drove over Echo Summit about nine. Everything seemed white and still against the sky. All of this was here before men were. Now, there are houses, cabins, towns, and roads about the hills and lakes of the Upper Sierras. I believe one sight of Lake Tahoe in the winter morning is worth creation. I can envy those who live there, who wake up to its brightness and its storms. But beauty depends in part upon whether we are ourselves warm, or at least this beauty does. We search for warmth, I think, especially when there is cold and snow and beauty about.

31. McLuhan once remarked, "To the sense of touch, all things are sudden, counter, original, strange."

VII

My niece had a black eye. "We had this experiment in class," she laughed, "in which we were supposed to experience what it is like to be blind. So my girl friend put a blindfold on me. She was supposed to guide me so I would not be hurt. I was trying to feel my way down the aisle. Suddenly, another girl came around the corner and turned sharply, only to run right into me. She didn't even receive a scratch. I have this black eye."

Yet, the sense of touch is not so harsh. Indeed, I think it is the most familiar, the warmest of all the senses. Sight does not replace it.

32. The fiftieth anniversary issue of *The Commonweal* reprinted an article of J. F. Powers, written in 1945, about Scott Fitzgerald. "As Fitzgerald matured — 'It's in the thirties that we want friends. In the forties, we know they won't save us any more than love did' — he discovered the prom room of his early dreams to be strangely empty of other people, a few only remained and not to dance. . . ."

This is quite true. Neither love nor friendship will save us. I once thought they would, but now I realize that it is the other way around. Love and friendship are the results of salvation, not the cause.

33. We do not have to be responsible for all problems of all men that come after us in time. This is why we die. We do not have to be responsible for all the problems before our time either. This is why we were born. Nonetheless, the present gives us some responsibility. I think though that being responsible is often recognizing that we are not responsible, not capable of doing so many things. This is why, I suggest, every so often, that we list all those things we shall never do, like play the violin for the Chicago Symphony Orchestra, fight for the Egyptian Army, walk on the Moon, run a co-op in Polynesia, or play rugby in Dunedin, New Zealand.

34. People who are harsh, or at least who once seemed harsh and foreboding, come sometimes to be seen as milder,

more pleasing than we expected. It is not that our initial judgments were necessarily unfair or unjust. But it makes us very cautious about the demand for instant joy or friendship. We are given time, I often think, to allow us to change our minds and our lives. We do not always change them for the better. This is why the past also judges us. This too is why there is drama all about us, why there is humor too.

35. "I love the picture of you on the couch with the phone, smiling and laughing, feet on the table. Typical teen-age boy in the boat, master of all he surveys, except that the boat does not look like it is in the water!" It wasn't either.

36. That we should be aware of the evil in ourselves is a very necessary quality in us. Look first at the beam in your own eye. But it is true that we cannot reduce all problems to self-reflection. In a real way, this sensibility for our own evil has been the cause of neglecting others. To proclaim that we too are evil can be a form of pride as well as a righteous reason for neglecting others.

Marcus Aurelius also said in the Seventh Book of his *Meditations*: "What is evil? It is something you have often seen. And whatever happens, keep this in mind, that it is something you have seen again and again. Everywhere up and down you will find the same things with which histories are filled, in the olden times, in medieval times, and today, repeating themselves in our cities and homes. There is nothing new; all things are familiar and quickly over" (VII, 67).

37. When you study politics formally or practice it professionally, you must be aware that your judgments will be disputed and rejected by the simplest and most ignorant of men. Furthermore, you will realize soon enough that simple and ignorant men are frequently correct. The fact that they are not always right is what makes us skeptical about pure democracy in any of its forms. Participation in rule, in other words, is not the formula for goodness. Aristotle saw this

very clearly. The lesson has not changed much except perhaps to add that all other forms of government also are composed of human beings who are subject to error and evil.

38. For the Twenty-Fifth and Last Sunday after Trinity, the Book of Common Prayer has this Collect: "Stir up, we beseech thee, O Lord, the wills of thy faithful people; that they, plenteously bringing forth the fruits of good works, may by thee be plenteously rewarded; through Jesus Christ our Lord, Amen."

At first sight, Christians are, unaccountably, pragmatic and selfish, wanting plenteous good works together with plenteous reward. They recognize the need of some divine prodding, of course; they are not Pelagians who think they can do it all themselves. Yet, it is somehow refreshingly right to read this Collect, to want to do good works for others, to have hope that we ourselves shall someday receive God's reward. Our faith is no abstraction. Ultimate happiness is something we expect to experience, even though we steadfastly realize it is not ours to give or achieve by ourselves.

39. In the beginning of the Book of *Revelation*, it says: "Blessed is he who reads aloud the words of prophecy. . . ." What I especially like to read aloud is *Daniel*:

> And to him was given dominion and glory and kingdom, that all peoples, nations, and languages should serve him; his dominion is an everlasting dominion, which shall not pass away, and his kingdom one that shall not be destroyed.

I also like to read aloud this from *Revelation:*

> Grace to you and peace from him who is and who was and who is to come.

Reading aloud does make a difference too somehow. Death

and evil have been defied with such words. Yet, we hardly dare to believe it, or say it.

40. What we receive is suited to our needs. We do not always know this. But lives do not have to be as they are. We receive them too.

VIII

Men exist for the sake of one another. Teach them or bear with them.
— Marcus Aurelius, Meditations, VIII, 59.

1. A friend, a librarian in Sunnyvale, California, showed me a wonderful old book, a collection of essays from *Vanity Fair*, written during the twenties and thirties, a book with men of the year, cartoons, essays by Benchley, Chesterton, Beerbohm, Dorothy Parker. The public library was throwing the book away, but it would not sell it or even give it away. They were going to destroy it. I felt annoyed. Old books should not die so. What kind of libraries do we now have, I wondered? And yet, my own book shelves are overcrowded.

Have you ever been in a home with no books? And still, books are not life or happiness, though they are not totally unconnected with them either. Michael Jackson once gave me an essay of Leo Strauss in which he said that the only way we can encounter the greatest minds that have ever lived is through books, that we are lucky if two or three of the great minds of mankind are alive during our own lifetimes.

2. "I am able to accept this 'problem' better day by day. So either I have a strong constitution or God loves me. I prefer to think it's the latter."

3. The university players were doing the musical ver-

sion of *Zorba the Greek*, a show I dearly love. I also saw it recently again in Los Angeles. I think I would see it any time I could. This line has never left me from *Zorba*: "Life is what you do while you're waiting to die." There is a profundity here. Life in death, death in life. Yet, it is not to be morbid. In *Zorba*, you dance while you're waiting to die; this makes the difference. C. S. Lewis says that you dance after you die too.

4. Samuel Johnson remarked: "Sir, you must not neglect doing a thing immediately good, from fear of remote evil; — from fear of its being abused." How sane this is. Is it possible that the fear of doing evil is itself evil? Still, the point is not about the status of evil, but of the good. There is a certain zest about life that reminds us that the world is well-made, despite all evidence to the contrary. We recognize, of course, that there is evidence to the contrary. We even suspect that this evidence too is for our benefit.

5. "I found the casinos at Lake Tahoe depressing in a way. I cannot stand to lose money — or anything else, for that matter." There is likewise a certain refreshment about people who cannot stand to lose. Our very attitude toward winning or losing seems to influence whether we win or lose, in fact, even by the strict laws of chance. I am always astonished at how often my own stepmother wins at bingo or in Reno.

Nevertheless, to be human means to lose sometimes. I would say that to be a Christian means that losers can be winners. He who loses his life shall save it. Yet Christianity insists on the possibility of absolute losers. This is God's risk in making us human or not at all. And it is this too that makes our existence a mysterious adventure, something Tolkien understood in his *Letters*, which I read with great fascination, after Bob Maloney told me where to buy them in a bookstore on Powell Street in San Francisco.

6. Sincerity is very devastating, for it is but a shade from pure selfishness. Indeed, it has come to be selfishness

under guise often. We have come to be told that the status of our self-conception guarantees interest or truth. All it usually guarantees is that we are mostly attentive to ourselves.

7. "I stood in line one day for almost twenty minutes at Warsaw's leading bakery to buy paczki; accomplished same and said brightly to John that night, 'Oh, I've got paczki from Blikle's for breakfast' — then sixty seconds (i.e., one minute) later, it occurred to me that I don't even like the damned things. I must have known subconsciously for a long time, but it struck me as being hysterically funny that I am such a sheep that I would stand in line to buy what-is-said-to-be-something-one-should-want-to-have."

The only other question, I suppose, is whether someone else might like the damned things. Then, it is all right to wait twenty minutes in line for them.

8. Should we do things we do not want to do, or not do things we want to do? Not easy this, always, to decide, but this is what humanity is all about. The question is not that I can do what I want to do, even though we should want, but sometimes I do not do what I want because I am sensitive to others, just because they are about.

9. Some things exist only to be beautiful. Perhaps all things.

10. At times, it is bound to happen that our feelings are hurt, that we hurt the feelings of others. It is not right to hope for a world in which such things won't happen, our hurting and being hurt. Therefore, we must discover riches, spiritual riches, if you will, that enable us· to accept hurtness, that give us the strength to see that the feelings of others do not always define their best interests, or even ours.

11. I tend to be for mildness at all costs. I know this is not always right. Yet, it is often right.

12. What is a great teacher? When I walked out of the classes of the best teacher I ever had, most of my companions said he was a terrible teacher.

Joe Fessio gave me this reflection of Dorothy Sayers:

"For the sole true end of education is simply this: to teach men how to learn for themselves; and whatever instruction fails to do this is effort spent in vain."

I read this to a class of ten on the first day of the fall semester. The next day, three dropped the class.

13. John Cage said in *Silence*: "When I was young, people told me: you'll see when you're fifty years old. Now I'm fifty. I've seen nothing."

For me, fifty is well in sight, looking backwards. When I was young, no one ever told me I would ever see everything. But I have seen a lot, I think. Probably, John Cage was right, though. I have really seen nothing. Saint Paul says something to this effect, the glass darkly.

The only thing to add to this, then, is this: I am a Christian. Therefore, I've seen nothing *yet*. But this only means that the wonder we have seen, and it has been real enough, is a mere shadow of a promise.

14. Mauriac said: "But I belong to that race of people who, born to Catholicism, realize in earliest manhood that they will be within it forever and ever. They are inundated with light; they know that it is true." Such types are rarer these days, I suppose, though Mauriac was right. Christians do exist who know that the Light shines in the Darkness. Should the Christian view of the world be essentially valid, the vision of most men, then, misses a lot. Perhaps this is why humility is such a basic virtue for the believer, why too so few have the capacity for joy in this vale of tears.

15. And there are tears. I said to a friend, "It is all right to cry." Laughter, however, as I think, requires more faith than tears. This is the unsettling truth. Laughter is related to faith. It would not be absolutely correct to say that God created the world so that we could laugh. But it would be largely correct. Though he created it so that we could cry too.

16. Belloc wrote a marvelous book about Paris in 1900. Reading it is an adventure, as all reading should be, recal-

ling my own brief visits to Paris, a city so wonderful, so overwhelming that it defied description. There is a map of the Seine Island in Roman times, before Notre Dame, of course. I remember sitting in the park at the back of this great structure, cool, late at night, the lights made all seem green. I was happy on that visit to Paris.

"From that time (A.D. 1000), our own Europe has never lost its eagerness, its abundant vigor, its power of expansion, and it has held in its mental attitude a spirit of inquiry — the spirit which Renan so admirably calls "la grande curiosité"—the basis of all our grandeur."

Curiosity is the basis of grandeur. I think that was why I was happy in Paris, a curiosity that revealed grandeur. I was astonished that so much could be given in our lives, and, as I was later to learn, so much taken away.

17. In Paris, I remember reading Cyril Connolly's *The Unquiet Grave*. I still have the boarding pass of the plane I left Rome on as a book mark in it. Connolly wrote, and I underlined, as I did so much of that book: "How many people drop in on us? That is the criterion of friendship. Or how many tell us our faults? To how many do we give unexpected presents? With whom do we remain silent?"

Surely these are right criteria. To me, the deepest one is that about unexpected presents. In my mail box was a note telling me to see John. I did. He took me down into the basement of Georgetown into the huge ice box. He gave me a package containing a cake and a note. It was from my Korean friend, an absolutely delicious cake, from nowhere, which I gave to the others at table, who all liked it very much, as it really was good.

Connolly continued: "Now that I seem to have obtained a temporary calm, I understand how valuable unhappiness can be." There was a sense of loss too about Paris, the losing of something I had only just begun to realize I could have.

18. It was the last day of November. Low fog was rolling over the City by the Bay. It was just getting light, though

you could see below the fog to the ocean. I love these shorter days of the year's end. We are in something of an eternal cycle, to be sure. Every year is astronomically pretty much the same, so that shorter and longer days, their effects on us, are more a question of our own moods. Yet, there is a kind of warmth and human closeness to shorter days.

To me, a storm on a late November day is one of the glories which we await with anticipation. Though the meteorological question is a fair one, and men are working furiously to learn to control the weather, still I hope they never do learn much. Weather is the abiding symbol of unexpectedness, the symbol that the expected does not ever quite happen, though I suppose I should qualify that, as I once read of the desert in Northern Chile, where it never rains. Too, I remember spending a week with Jim and Sheila in Nairobi, where the sun always went down at 6 o'clock, all year around. It was very unsettling to me, somehow, this absolute regularity.

19. Rain is not something you always should come in out of.

20. *The Literary Digest Atlas* I bought for a dime, as I said, was published the year after I was born. It is clearly a rather old book now. In those years, evidently, the great adventure was not space but Anarctica, a place we seldom hear of any more, except to be told it is polluted. But once it was the ultimate adventure of mankind to reach the South Pole. This mankind has need of ultimate adventures.

21. On a rainy day walk, with sopping wet clothes, you suddenly discover that your skin is waterproof.

22. Emerson wrote: "Every actual state is corrupt. Good men must not obey the laws too well." This is, of course, quite true. Plato said much the same thing. But perhaps it would be better to say that much corruption exists in every state. Therefore, we should be wary of obeying laws that are tainted.

23. On a clear, chilly day in December, the grass in

Golden Gate Park was very moist, wet. A group of Chinese and Mexican children were playing kickball on the green field. They had just been thrown off the muddy infield by their teacher and the park gardeners.

Over at the children's playground, which forbids you to visit "Unless Accompanied by Children," I walked through anyhow, because a law must not be obeyed too well. There was a big chicken coop in the middle of the playground — full of roosters, hens of all sorts. I presume most city children would never have seen a live chicken were it not for this domestic zoo.

While I watched, a boy of about nine jumped over the fence and was creeping slowly up on an unsuspecting hen. Suddenly, a sharp yell from the chicken coop froze him: "Get out of here!" So city boys even have the thrill of being caught.

Just as I was about to pass into the tunnel under Stanyan Street, or the street before it in the park, three young black girls called back an old white man, a real down-and-out type, who had evidently just asked them for a handout. He came trotting back. "Here's a dime, Mister." He thanked them. He wore tennis shoes, one arm seemed partly paralyzed, probably an alcoholic, an old sports coat, white hair, maybe sixty-five or so. He then walked fairly quickly over to the grocery store just outside the park, though I do not know what he could have bought with a dime. He was collecting, I guessed.

"What nice girls," I thought. He had evidently touched something in them, and they responded. Such a world is rather nice to live in, I think.

24. Loneliness is not something to be sorry about. In fact, as I have said, it is usually healthy, a reminder that we are not where we want to be, with whom we want to be. And this is so even when we are where we want to be, with whom we want to be.

25. Rejoice that you learned something that you really

did not have to know. Or better, be glad that there are multitudes of things that need not be known, but yet may be and are delightful.

26. " 'Aunt Ann, do you think animals go to heaven?' asks little Katie (niece), while we were making the salad for last night's party at her mom and dad's (brother's) house. 'People disagree on that. What do you think?' 'I think, if I were God, I would want all of my creation with me.' *Isn't that an extraordinary statement from a 4th grader!* So we finished the salad and then painted our nails and gabbed. She is a wonderful child."

27. So I did see *Zorba the Greek*, once as a movie, once as a college play in San Francisco, once at the Dorothy Chandler Pavillion in Los Angeles, roughly at ten-year intervals. "She's all right, she's dying!" The production in college lacked the attention to food and eating that it had in the book, which I have also read several times.

"What is this world? I wondered. What is its aim and in what way can we help to attain it during our ephemeral lives? The aim of man and matter is to create joy, according to Zorba. . . ." The whole question is, of course, how do these two sentiments co-exist — the being all right while dying, creating joy? Yet, they do fit together.

28. Often, you can only begin when you begin again.

29. Jacques Ellul noted in *The Political Illusion*: "The lover united with his beloved never writes poems; poetry is produced only as a result of absence and loss. Poetry is only a verbal affirmation of love when love is no longer anything but a cloud, a regret, anxiety attacking the individual's uncertainty." I am not much prepared to believe, however, that a happy lover never writes poems. But it is so that absence and loss remind us of the essential things, things lost, or those never gained. I believe too that contented love is probably more poignant than absence or even loss. He who does not sense this does not love in a human way.

30. For many problems, there are no solutions. But I do not think this is a pessimistic statement.

31. Monte was telling us of a stuffy professor of canon law who came out from the East, whom they affectionately called in class, "Arizona Reid." "Why that?" I asked. "Because he was clear and dry." To quote my friend, "I love bad jokes." But that was a pretty good way of describing the class. One of the best things about our humanity is our capacity to laugh at our foibles and stuffiness. For me, there is now no way to forget "Arizona Reid."

32. When friends settle in a world we really do not personally know, it is painful and alienating in some ways. Yet, we want our friends to have their own world, which oftentimes cannot include us. The world is so much larger than our circle of friends. Indeed, any real group of friends must be rather narrow. It takes so much time. This means that many loves, many friendships we shall never know. But it also means that there are some friends we can actually have.

33. I came across a book of Japanese reflections written about 1330, called "Essays in Idleness." This is what I copied down. "If a man were never to fade away like the dews of Adashino (a cemetery), never to vanish like the smoke over Toribeyama (another cemetery), but lingered on forever in the world, how things would lose their power to move us. The most precious thing in life is its uncertainty." We need little more than this to prove our common humanity across nations and the ages. The most precious thing in life is its uncertainty. I believe this, for it means that we choose our world, our lives are not planned. They are full of surprises.

34. Zorba said to the crime of killing the widow — leave her alone, nothing can now be done about it. There are things best left alone, at least best left alone by us. It is, after all, a form of madness to want to experience absolutely everything. In this sense, we are what we select. In *The*

Republic, Plato raised the question of punishment for crimes that could not be punished in this life. It is not for us to right all wrongs. Some things must be left to go their own ways. It is poignant but not tragic that others pass by, that others pass on.

35. Men exist for the sake of one another. The young woman's roommate had serious mental problems. She felt it her duty to assist her, but the task was ruining her composure, her work, her balance.

"You cannot do what you are incapable of doing," I told her, somewhat too abstractly. "If her doctors cannot help, advisors, clergy, family, and normal friendships do not work, your task is to leave her. Her only cure may depend on something else."

To exist for the sake of one another means that sometimes we cannot help. This is a humility we must all eventually accept. We are none of us capable of aiding all those we meet or who need help. Oftentimes, our best friends will be beyond our reach. Providence thus says to us, "You are not the only person in the world." And this is our ultimate joy.

IX

All things are the same, familiar, ephemeral, worth-
less; everything is now just as it was in the time of
those whom we have buried.
    – Marcus Aurelius, Meditations, IX, 14.

1. In *One Dimensional Man*, Herbert Marcuse says:
"Critical thought strives to define the irrational character of
the established rationality...." Yet, is there no wonder to the
established rationality also? Is it not better to begin here? I
am uneasy about the incapacity to appreciate what is, even
though there may be much wrong with it. I distrust people
who begin their search for reality within their own minds.

2. December in the hills down the Peninsula in the
Santa Cruz Mountains is full of low fog, haze. All is green,
obscure. How much we cannot see, even when we see.

3. We often do not know how to help. Likewise, we often
do not know how to receive aid when we ourselves need it.
The giving and the receiving are both needs in the world.
These surely make it a more loving world, both.

4. My cousin Shirley called from the airport. She was
flying through. I was glad she called. I had not expected it.
Her father, my Uncle Tom, died years ago, in Des Moines, I
think. I can remember Uncle Tom showing movies of the

great snowstorm of 1936 in Pocahontas County, where I was born.

5. All the time I was in her hospital room, I knew I would cry. She did not yet know how serious her cancer was. Her small children, her family were there. I had never seen her children before. Her hair was cut short. She laughed because some psychologist had said women with short hair were aggressive.

"Why do I have to come to the hospital to see you?" she asked.

"I thought of you lately," I answered. "I found Belloc's book on *Paris*, and I even saw Montmarte from the Orient Express on the way to London. May I come back in a couple of days, you may feel better. I would like to read some of *Paris* to you."

"I would like that," she said.

Actually, I wanted to read to her Belloc's "A Remaining Christmas," but I was afraid to, as I feared it would be too sad, both as Christmas was near and as I was not yet sure how serious her illness was.

Yet, I wanted to read it to her.

Man has a body as well as a soul, and the whole of man, soul and body, is nourished sanely by a multiplicity of observed traditional things. Moreover, there is this great quality in the unchanging practice of Holy Seasons, that makes explicable, tolerable and normal what is otherwise a shocking and intolerable and even in the fullest sense, abnormal thing. I mean the mortality of immortal man.

Yes, she should have heard it. She would have understood, especially if I also had read a fairy tale, perhaps something in *The Chronicles of Narnia* would be best, or maybe something like *The Unquiet Grave*, which I had read to her before. The doctor, in the end, forbade any exertion, even reading. She recovered somewhat for a time. Then she died.

6. We were driving near Five Wounds, the old, baroque Portuguese Church in San Jose in California, a church I had never entered, I, who have seen St. Peter's, Santa Croce, Rheims, Santa Maria Gloriosa, Cologne, Kyoto, the Bath Abbey, Chichester, and St. Nicholas in Bari, have never seen Five Wounds in my own back yard.

Jim had said in the midst of his driving, when the question was still current: "How can you tell Nixon is lying?" "I give up," I answered. "When his lips are moving," came his dry reply. I could not help but be glad at silly laughter in my hometown, going by one of its traditional places I shall never see. Like the rest of life, it seemed to gain in fascination; even cruel jokes are funny. They say that in totalitarian societies, that is all that is left for the self-defense of the people — cruel jokes.

7. "Call Clara, would you?" Bill asked me earnestly. "Tell her Nancy had a massive stroke. She is dying, right now. I just came from the hospital." Strange days of sadness. I called Clara. She had not yet known. "But I just saw her at noon, she seemed a bit offish, but we chatted, are you sure you have the right person?"

I was sure. I told her about my other friend. "That is why I always say," Clara reflected, "that you should live each minute to the fullest."

And Clara was mostly right, I thought. Yet, such sickness forces us, too, to other questions, not just to live to the fullest, though we should do that too. And how is it our loves and lives do not end — *the mortality of immortal men*.

8. Sometimes when we need the strength of consolation, metaphysical, even divine strength, for our shock that we are indeed mortal, there is no place to turn but to music or to stories.

Charles Williams is a good choice:

"I don't know why," he said, "but how is clear enough. These cards are in touch with a thing I'll

show you at Christmas, and they are in touch with
... well, there aren't any words for it — with the
Dance."
"The Dance?" she asked.
"The Dance that is ... everything," he answered.

This is an ever recurring notion in Williams, C. S. Lewis,
and Tolkien, that the cosmos is a great Dance we are invited
to participate in, that it is already going on.

Williams continued:

"With eyes that necessarily veiled their passion,
she saw in her niece the opening of some other abyss
in that first abyss which was love. Mr. Coningsby had
spoken more truly than he thought when he accused
Sybil of an irresponsibility not unlike Nancy's; their
nature answered each other across the years. But
between them lay the experience of responsibility,
that burden which is only given in order to be relinquished, that task put into the hands of man in order
that his own choice may render it back to its creator,
that yoke which, once wholly lifted and put on, is
immediately no longer to be worn."

Some other abyss in the first abyss. Yes, that is it, isn't it?
All love leads to this second abyss, the Great Dance, the
mortality of immortal men.

9. What is given is given to be given back. Each word is
important. What is first given really need not be given.
What is given back really need not be given back. The cycle
of the world consists in this: responsibility taken up is then
relinquished. We are not alone. The Great Dance goes on.

10. My friends in San Jose have lived in a couple of
wonderful houses. Their first one had a large yard, full of
fruit trees, oranges, grapefruit, lemons, flowers, arbors, old
sheds, and gardens. There were dogs and cats. "Did you hear
Dan's frog croak in your room last night?" Jim laughed.

Dinner was always a surprise there, full of conversation, not too serious, light, warm as meals should mostly be. The children have always been favorites of mine, creative, dear. They have grown. I was the celebrant at Dan's wedding in the Mission Church at Santa Clara.

My stepmother and I were over for breakfast one Sunday morning. She said to them, "I can now see why my son spends so much time over here."

11. When something is very good, we should admit that it is. Excellence can be a tyranny, but it is also the highest compliment we can give to our friends. I read *In Pursuit of Excellence*. Its thesis seemed to be that what the poor depend on most is excellence in the excellent.

12. A couple of years ago, just before I returned to Rome for the ninth time, someone said to me, "Rome is probably no longer the same to you now that so many of your friends are no longer there." Yet, Rome was always the same to me. "Things happen there in a more intense way," someone told me once. And that was always true for me. Cities are places wherein we would know one another. That is what they are.

Rome was always a city of remembrance. We go back when many of our friends are gone. We go and friends stay. New friends, we hope, will always be given to us. And the beauty, the haunting beauty remained to enchant us, to disturb us. Why is it so often, I wonder, that we have to be without friends to discover beauty, even the beauty and kindness of our friends. Yet, I have not returned to Rome for several years now. When friends ask, "Don't you want to go back, even for a visit?" I say, "No, one cannot visit such a place. I am content where I am."

13. Augustine insisted on believing that the only division among men that counted was the one between those who chose good and those who chose evil. And he did not attribute this to our own powers, this distinction, or not exclusively so. It is very humbling to believe Augustine was

right. And it is difficult to show where he was wrong. Indeed, he was not wrong.

14. In the First Book of the *Chronicles of Narnia*, which is called *The Lion, the Witch, and the Wardrobe*, it says: "People who have not been in Narnia sometimes think that a thing cannot be good and terrible at the same time." We are never to forget this. I wonder if this is why salvation was "according the flesh," to enable us to see the good through the terror of the Cross, to prevent us from rejecting what we should very much want, were we to persist in our own confidences. To be good must ultimately involve to believe.

15. Sincerity, I believe, is the least of the virtues and perhaps the most insidious of all. For it is the one that substitutes for the good, an internal and subjective feeling as its main mark and justification.

16. Samuel Hazo wrote a rather good poem entitled, "On the Metroliner, I remember that to be is to remember." I have been on this Metroliner from New York to Trenton.

But the sentiment of the title is not quite true. To be is rather to have *something* to remember, and though we may want to blot them out, this includes our faults and sins and foolishnesses. Nonetheless, I think the greatest burden of memory lies rather in the nice things that happen. For the good is much harder to bear than the evil.

17. What moves us, the deeds of our lives, those of others, these need to be reflected upon, even brooded on a bit. We are in danger ever of trivialization. "An unreflected life is not worth living . . ." — this is what began our civilization.

18. "Really liked your scrapbook, mixed-media approach to letter-writing. 'Vasistas,' I knew — 'was ist das?' Your picture (of the boulangerie) made me more than ever long for the sights and smells of Paris. Have you ever felt a great swelling lump (not the cancerous kind) of nostalgia build up inside of you? What I wouldn't give to be trans-

ported there — even an hour sitting on a park bench in the Jardin du Luxembourg. . . .

"I do wish my doctors weren't so grouchy about visitors. Feeling that healing is their private domain, they simply won't tolerate competition from spiritual healers.

"My son had the audacity to cut his first two teeth in my absence; I shall never forgive him for getting along without me. — If I don't get home soon, they'll all realize how dispensible I am.

"Sister Irene, my fourth grade religion teacher, promised that God would never send more misery than he thought you could handle. Somehow, he has grossly overrated me. The next couple of days will be filled with tests and treatments, a dreary thought. My prayers and thoughts for a joyful Christmas."

What to say? Sister Irene's theology is correct enough in the long run. In fact, I said, "Probably God gives us suffering mainly for others."

At her funeral, they prayed mainly for others. I said to Mike, "At my funeral, I hope they pray mainly for me."

19. Do not be too hard on other people's casualness. It is a protection too. Did you ever read James Thurber? Humor is melancholic too, burdened with the deep sadness of things.

20. "To have to tell someone what you need — it's degrading. I wish someone would guess. But people are too casual." How difficult it is to help and to be helped when we need it. Yet, to tell someone what we need is an honor to them. We can, I think, also hurt people by refusing to accept their help, a small point, but worth some thought.

21. I do not think that all people can do more than they themselves think they can, though I am sure most can. Some

99

people, however, are fatheads who can do considerably less than they think they can. This is not the problem of most people. Most people, in fact, lack confidence in what they can do. Encouragement of others is a sort of beatitude.

God created each person unique. None is repeatable. Aquinas said that God loved us before we existed, that is why we were created. I believe that.

22. To every question, there is not necessarily an answer. But that is all right. I should hate a world in which everything was answered, a world with no adventure, no risk.

23. We must learn to live with small insights and many partial answers, most of which are wrong.

24. It is a kind of pride to believe others are happier or more fortunate or more content than we are, just as it is a bit of a perversion to want to live some life other than our own.

25. In the *Chronicle of Current Events*, that most useful and effective record of events in the Soviet Union, I read:

> On July 26, 1972, the paper *Evening Tbilisi* published an interview with the Rector of the Pushkin Pedagogical Institute in Tbilisi, Natala Vasadze. It included, among other things, the following comment: *Correspondent*: 'At a recent Plenum of the City Council one of your teachers was criticized for performing religious ceremonies in church.' *Rector*: 'We sacked her. How can a person who adheres to superstition be an educator of youth?' (Teacher of English Megi Rezheradze had been seen lighting a candle in church on Easter Eve.)

I had never been especially drawn to candle lighting in church. Perhaps there is more to be said for it than I had suspected.

San Francisco columnist Herb Caen told of a sign in a Southern Church which said: "If they were persecuting

Christians, would they find enough evidence to convict you?"
Perhaps this is why we need candles, to keep our faith from
being only a thought, with no evidence of it.

27. Epicurus: "Laws are enacted for the sake of the wise,
not that they may do wrong, but that they may suffer no
wrong." This is valid in a way. We need to allow the wise wide
scope to be wise, even though part of wisdom must have to do
with suffering wrong, suffering it often from those we think
wise.

28. In *August 1914*, Solzhenitsyn described an advanced
lady school directress, whom he rather liked: "She and her
late husband had regarded it as the chief aim of education to
bring up young people as citizens — that is to say, as individuals with an inherent mistrust of authority."

We should not obey all laws too well. Would that it were
factual that the wise citizens were always known to be also
good. Chesterton said that the belief in original sin alone
made democracy possible, alone allowed us to say why we
could not always trust the powerful and the rich.

29. In a used book store on Clement Street, a friend found
a copy of Ben Shahn's marvelous edition of *Ecclesiastes*.
Chapter Nine began, not unlike Marcus Aurelius, yet differently too:

> For all this I considered in my heart even to declare
> all this, that the righteous, and the wise, and their
> works, are in the hands of God: No men knoweth
> either love or hatred by all that is before them. All
> things are alike to all: There is one event to the
> righteous, and to the wicked; to the good and to the
> clean, and to the unclean; to him that sacrificeth, and
> to him that sacrificeth not: as is the good, so is the
> sinner; and he that sweareth, as he that feareth an
> oath. This is an evil among all things that are done
> under the sun, that there is one event unto all: yes,
> also the heart of the sons of men is full of evil, and

madness is in their heart while they live, and after
they go to the dead.

This is the difference, of course, even tragedy and evil are in
some way also in the hands of God, their reconciliation, at
least.

30. This is the Second Day of a New Year, my sister's
birthday. We are already into the last years of this century.
The curious problem of our age, at least to itself, is that its
crises and problems, its joys and its sins are too unique to be
in the hands of God. *Ecclesiastes* has said that we are out-
wardly all alike in joys and sorrows given to us. Reality
refuses to reward automatically the good for their goodness,
nor yet to return evil to the evil.

This century demands a sign, and no sign is given to it.

Therefore, we are free.

Therefore, we are somewhat sad.

X

Point by point, whenever we do anything, let us pause and ask ourselves if death is a dreadful thing because it deprives us of all this.
– Marcus Aurelius, Meditations, X, 29.

1. The special bus to the casino at Lake Tahoe took me to my brother's at about half price and much more quickly. The bus was about to leave the San Francisco terminal on an early winter morning, chilly, wet. I was sixth in line. Two elderly couples from New York were ahead of me. The man first in line was in Levi's, white hair, strong, friendly. He told the couples that he made the trip often. He explained just how it worked, the refunds the casinos give, the return bus. He was, he said, "a professional gambler."

He next looked at me several times, as if I were to confirm his observations. "I've seen you before on this trip a thousand times. You know how it works," he addressed me. "I'm sorry, but I only have been on this bus a couple of times before in my life; I use it to see my brother." "Well, I'm mixed up. You must look like someone I know who is always gambling near me."

It is not unusual to be taken for someone else. Yet, we

103

do not want to be someone else, really. This is our glory. We are only ourselves.

2. Death does deprive us of many dear and wonderful things. No one can doubt this, for to do so would make our commitments and efforts tepid and meaningless. We cannot make the death of any loved one more tolerable by making the thing lost to be of little value. This is what the abortionists do regularly. Christianity is a disturbing faith because it insists that our little world, the things we discover in it, are near to infinity. Yet, they still pass on. This is why Christianity is also a promise.

3. Dom David Knowles wrote of the long years of his life, in which he tried to understand the changes that have taken place:

> This frame of mind, hostile to any way of life which in one way or another was guided by standards, values and "essences" outside of the individual, was irked by constraint of any kind, whether of law or of dogma. In the last analysis, existentialist and individualist thought is inconsistent with any creator, whose design and will can be known by human creatures even without direct revelation, and in whose will, and there alone, is peace.

There is something very important and even paradoxical here, that our own laws do not give us peace. The great challenge we face constantly is that the world is better made than we might give it credit for, but not by our standards.

5. One January morning, I was listening to the news which announced that Tex Ritter, the cowboy singer and actor, had died in Nashville. I have been in Nashville a bit. Indeed, I once read a book called *The Nashville Sound*, which my cousin gave me:

> Tex Ritter is alive and doing very well, thank you, in Nashville. The 78 cowboy movies he made between

1936 and 1948 seem like ancient history to him, and he has to think a while to remember the names of any of them. Now he is sixty-five years old, with two sons in college, and he and his wife live in a rambling, unpretentious ranch-style home at Franklin Road, near the old Hank Williams homestead. His schedule leaves him little time for reminiscing: playing the Opry on Saturday nights, when he's in town, working some 100 one-nighters a year like the youngsters do, raking in the royalties from all the hit songs he has had ("High Noon," "Rye Whisky," "The Wayward Wind," "Boll Weevil," et al.), taking care of business interests. . . . He is one of the best-liked entertainers within the Nashville music family, a good natured old-codger with the sonorous voice of an earnest country preacher. ("One night I dreamed I'd died, and I'll be a son of a bitch if it wasn't Tex giving my eulogy," said one Opry regular. . . .)

I neglected to visit Tex Ritter's grave when I was in Nashville or to listen again to a "High Noon." Tex Ritter, no longer alive and well in Nashville, the world seems less dreadful to me because he sang sentimental cowboy songs for us all at our eulogies.

6. In the Fifth Chapter of Ben Shahn's *Ecclesiastes*, it says: "If thou seest the oppression of the poor, and the violent perverting of judgment and justice in a province, marvel not at the matter: for he that is higher than the highest regardeth. . . ." The lack of this sense of divine awareness about the condition of the poor and persecuted is, I think, what gives politics its violence today. We believe that we must also accomplish the vengeance as well as the justice. And this burden is too great for us.

7. Part of Robert Nye's Poem, "Between":

Somewhere between Idea and Angel
We make our way,

X

Half dream, half shadow,
Angelic intellectual ghosts
Who can bleed.[9]

Our bleeding is what makes us miss things, what prevents our ideas from being only ideas.

8. Mauriac said: "A writer is essentially a man who will not be resigned to solitude. Each of us is like a desert, and a literary work is like a cry from the desert. . . . The point is: to be heard — even by one single person."

To be alone and to be heard, neither is possible without the other. Indeed, the more difficult thing to discover is solitude. We cannot really be ourselves without some degree of it. This is what these pages are about. Surely it is true that for many, life is a being cut off, a feeling of waste and depressive loneliness. God is other in his very being, and we are his image even in this, especially in this. Our solitude cannot always be broken lest we fail to hear what is to be heard.

9. No joy is more welcome than that discovered at the end of a confused, solitary journey across various frontiers and languages, on sighting friends there waiting. Solitude is not only discovered when others are absent. I do not believe people we love are ever fully absent. Yet, there is in us a need to see them again. This may, indeed, be the deepest need we have, the one that comes closest to a human proof of the need for resurrection.

10. Mauriac also said: "The greatest agony a man can experience is to survey his past from middle age and to realize that he has not been the master of his own life." Though I am indeed in middle age, this does not seem quite so. The greatest agony rather is memory, a walk down Clement Street, a visit to New Harmony, sitting on Rio del Mar Beach, the children on Christmas morning, seeing Constable's *Salisbury Cathedral* in the National Gallery in Wash-

9. *The Tablet*, December 8, 1973.

ington, then seeing it years later in Salisbury, then seeing the painting again. The one grace is that we are not masters of our own lives. Therefore, something new can be given to us. Aristotle said that trifles are the beginnings of revolution. They are also the beginnings of our loves and joys. Perhaps that is what he meant, that our very lives are revolutions.

11. "I arrived home from the hospital only to realize in dismay how well everyone has fared without me. One good thing — I can still love. I'm in love with my little son. He's so beautiful."

"I replied, 'No, that is not correct. They did not fare well without you. They survived, perhaps, but that is not the same thing.'

12. "Today is the second of a four-day retreat . . . a contemplative one, meaning, I do not get lectured at. Lots of time for prayer and reflection. My usually overbearing self literally 'eats up' this time of quiet and solitude.

"It is snowing outside — it has been for two days straight. As I look out the window, I see some of the loveliest country Wisconsin has to offer, the bluffs and hills surrounding the Wisconsin River. Nothing is found for miles around the monastery. Some few farmhouses are set between the hills, pine covered valleys and hills, with a brook running in and out, and again snow, the perfect kind for long walks — nothing, no noises, except the quarter-hourly monastery bells sounding over the rises, a rooster, wild geese, flocks of birds, and, oh yes, the wind and the brook, sometimes louder, sometimes softer, depending on how close it comes to the road.

"The monastery building is mostly of logs and blends in with the environment. All is harmony. The birds come close to feed outside the living-room window, so do the deer. Rumor has it that the opossum and rodent-type critters show up too.

"I guess sometimes I travel so long and so hard that I

need a bit of time like this to pause and consider the map — where am I going?"

I can envy a friend who has been in a Wisconsin place in the dead of winter, someone who can pause, in a life that became much more difficult later.

13. Every day is as much the Omega as the Alpha, the End, the Beginning. That is why days come to an end, so that there will be something else other than what has been.

14. On a January afternoon, once, packing to return to Rome, I found an old letter:

> As you see, I am back to Freiburg, which in a way gave me a nice welcome. The weather was just as fine as it was when we took our long and exhausting (I'm afraid) walk three weeks ago. So I spent the first day taking another walk — the same direction. Just at the moment I feel it a bit difficult to be here after two weeks among my family. It is strange and a bit depressing to spend evenings in a room like this. But this is not supposed to be another mood-letter, though, if you don't mind too much, this might occur as well sometimes.

All letters we receive from friends, I think, are "mood-letters," ones which tell us sometimes directly, sometimes indirectly, how they are.

15. I had given a copy of my little book, *Play On*, with the cartoons I like so much, to a sick friend — both because I wanted it to cheer, as I thought it might, and because I wanted my friend to like it.

"Your book made me angry. Such an idea could come only from a spectator. That is my main position, probably an unfair one. Tell me why it makes me angry. I think it is because I'm envious. I'd like to be a spectator too."

Something sent to cheer, something of yours, angers, why? I said, "I think I understand. . . ." But I did not explain because my friend was telling me that death is a dreadful thing because it does deprive us of all these lovely things, hence the envy. Yet, we are still equally spectators, people who watch a world, a history, a providence, a love. We are saved by being also deprived.

16. In Claude Lelouche's film, *Happy New Year*, the man said, "Man is someone who risks everything." This is strange, for this is rather my definition of God. Perhaps, then God was a man, at least once upon a time, dwelling among us.

17. Out my window one late September afternoon, five girls were playing touch football against one boy. The boy was winning.

18. One of the most famous phrases of Samuel Johnson was the one about the Devil being a Whig. I had never seen the full context of this statement before, a statement which has a delight all its own.

> Boswell: "I drank chocolate, sir, this morning with Mr. Eld; and, to my no small surprise, found him to be a Staffordshire Whig, a being which I did not believe had existed." Johnson: "Sir, there are rascals in all countries." Boswell: "Eld said, a Tory was a creature generated between a non-juring parson and one's grandmother." Johnson: "And I have always said, the first Whig was the Devil." Boswell: "He certainly was, sir. The Devil was impatient of subordination; he was the first who resisted power."

The Devil, to be sure, did not resist power, but rather love, quite a different thing.

19. Santa Barbara is a lovely, old city along the California coast, a very lush, well-cared for place which accepts its beauty and its tradition as if it were natural and normal. My nephew and nieces went to college there. The Mission church is splendid. The plaza in front of it overlooks the ocean below with the Channel Islands in the distance. There is, to be sure, no necessary relation between physical beauty

and inner contentment. Yet, we must strive for some harmony, even if only symbolic, between the two. Inner peace should have some tangible effect on the world, some way to make it more beautiful. And the world can be made more beautiful. This is an ultimate mystery of man.

20. On a bright January day once, returning to Rome by a various route, I was in Albuquerque. The mountains were said to be some eighty miles away, but they seemed so close. The desert was all about. The nearness of Mexico was most evident. Albuquerque, though, had the ordered logic of the modern automobile-oriented city. Few homes were higher than one story. I walked through Old Town, downtown, into the Zoo, a sort of homey, ramshackle place with tiny children intently watching the animals.

One little boy of two or three exclaimed to his grandmother: "Look at the Jagwires!" His grandmother corrected him, "That's a leopard." The boy then watched the crows in the trees, about the only native species about. "I love those birds," he cried out earnestly.

I then walked across the Rio Grande Bridge nearby, a shallow, muddy sort of a river was below it. Every city is its own world in a way. Each has its own traditions; lives are lived and pass away in each one.

21. In Nashville, I was invited to a recording studio. Three country music numbers were put together and recorded in a couple of hours. Out of what did not exist, a song was formed, reformed, reformed again until someone said, "That's it." There was a completion. And you could not help but feeling that the conclusion was right. That was the way the song should be played. So completion is part of a beginning. There are some completions which then begin. And things that thus begin can begin again. A recording is something that can begin again. Not all things that delight us are things which we have never heard or done before.

The songs I heard recorded in Nashville I never heard

again, except for one. I heard it in a book store in Dar-es-Salaam in Tanzania, in Africa. How different it sounded in Nashville and in Africa. I never did learn how they got it there.

22. I do not believe in a parsimonious world. There are friends and relatives whose depth and beauty and intelligence and generosity are so overwhelming that we can only react with a kind of awe. If we react with envy, it is because we only want our own world.

23. The people I ran across in Nashville charmed, simple people. There was a lady in a curio shop across from the famous Tootsie's Orchid Bar (I wonder if it is still standing?), who told us of the Opry, the crowds, how she did not like Jesus people. One young man came into her shop, she related, and grabbed the somewhat lurid trick joke packets she had. "The Lord told me to take these away," he told her. She snatched them back, "Well, the boss tells you to leave them alone."

At a sandwich shop called "Mary's," a very dear black lady, partly crippled, I think, showed us to a place. "What'll you all have now?" "Have you any good sandwiches?" I asked. "What kind do you want?" I decided on a ham and cheese.

When she returned with it, she said with a warm smile, "I think you're gonna like that." After but one delicious bite, I told her, "It is already the best sandwich I have ever had." And it was. When we left, she said, "Now you'all come back again real soon, hear?"

The elderly lady at the cash register at an International House of Pancakes, where we had gone only for a cup of coffee, was also quite memorable. The coffee was served in huge cups, big enough for two or three normal cups. She was awkward and pleasantly apologetic. We had to leave after the first sip to go to the recording studios.

As I paid the bill, she said, "You mean you're gonna

leave us so soon? Why, I thought we were gonna have the pleasure of your company for a real long time, three or four cups."

I had never heard time measured by cups of coffee before. The world seemed better that day.

24. Time always passed rapidly on returning to Rome. Suddenly, I would find it was April. Rome seemed familiar again. One morning, I arose early and walked out into the dawn streets yet quiet. I climbed the long steps into the Church of the Ara Coeli. The light was just right for seeing Pinturicchio's magnificent "Glory and Death of Saint Bernadine of Siena," in the back corner chapel. It was in fact a few hours after the death of Georges Pompidou, then President of France, so the painting seemed somehow appropriate. The death of a public figure necessarily bids us pause for a moment. In the painting, the people of Siena seemed to stand still in their city, struck in thought. Four monks carried Bernadine, a passingness, yet a beauty too.

I went on to the Aventine. The flowering plums were in bloom. Vast vistas of the city, vast vistas of the past were everywhere. There was Santa Sabina, where Aquinas once had a room, then the Headquarters of the Knights of Malta, and Santa Prisca.

I walked back through the Campidoglio, by the great equestrian statue of Marcus Aurelius yet again. All morning, I had been brooding over Alexander Solzhenitsyn's "Letter to the Soviet Leaders," which a friend had sent me from London. What bothered me about Solzhenitsyn was his unreserved castigation of cities as such. Cities are like tumors and cancers, he said.

Yet, I could not help thinking as I looked up at Marcus Aurelius that death would not be dreadful because it deprived us of all the beauty he gazed at down those steps before him in Rome, but still to be deprived of our cities and their beauty is a fundamental loss. But then, that is the whole point. The beauty of all these things is real enough, and we acknowledge it. The world and its cities are much more poignant places when we realize their loveliness.

XI

Fourth, consider that you also do many things wrong, that you are a man like others; and even if you abstain from certain faults, you still have the disposition to commit them (even) though either through cowardice, or concern for reputation, or some such motive, you refrain from doing them.
    – Marcus Aurelius, Meditations, XI, 18.

1. Many years ago, I bought the *Autobiography of Benjamin Franklin*, but I never read it in the meantime. Every once in a while, I had looked at it, and I knew that someday I would get around to reading it. So I finally did. It turned out to be such a marvelous book. I was glad I saved it and hope the world is full of such saved things. There are so many wonderful stories in it — the nun in the garret in London, the conduct of Braddock's troops, Franklin's first visit to Philadelphia, his inventions.

Franklin was open and simple. Today, we read his project for improving our lives with considerable wonder. "It was about this time I conceived the bold and arduous project of arriving at moral perfection." He then set out to achieve this perfection in a rational way, listing the vir-

115

tues he though he ought to have, dividing up the time to achieve each, marking each step of progress in a book.

This is, of course, very similar to Ignatius of Loyola's proposed plan, which I have naturally tried, not reaching perfection yet, myself. Franklin felt that the reason we do not improve is because we do not work seriously enough at it. Finally, after some experiment, he remarked: "I was surpris'd to find myself so much fuller of faults than I had imagined; but I had the satisfaction of seeing them diminish."

It takes a bold man to define moral perfection — Franklin listed thirteen virtues he felt were required. But I must confess that I am delighted by the ingenuousness of Ben Franklin's surprise at finding himself with more faults than he expected. I suppose we all should be so astonished were we brave enough to examine the case.

2. I was telling a Canadian friend, who had studied in England, of my visit to Salisbury, a visit I made, as I have mentioned, because of once having seen John Constable's painting of this cathedral in the National Gallery. The beauty of the painting and the actual beauty of Salisbury itself on a June day made me wonder about creativity, about the fact that one beautiful place can inspire another fully beautiful thing now such a long way away. Sitting in the park before the cathedral near the Avon, gazing at its lofty spire across the grass, it is surely one of the world's most beautiful sights.

Heinrich Boll wrote an essay in *The Sunday Times* called, "Attitudes and Anglo-Saxons": "Something else, too, which may be so obvious to the English eye that it passes unnoticed: there is hardly a country in Europe where spring and autumn are so beautiful — and beautiful in an authentically English way — from the many daffodils (too many as far as I am concerned) to the ancient beech trees in the park."

Is it a fault not to recognize beauty, I wonder?

3. "Yes," I said, "you cannot always be too frank. You

cannot call every bastard, a bastard. Some bastards cannot bear it. And that is all right. Often, the only way we can acknowledge our faults is to go on living."

4. Sandra was quoted in a local British newspaper as saying: "Theatre like this is a useful way of showing people situations they know nothing about." I liked that. Indeed, I always try to tell students to read or write about something they know nothing about.

Sandra was about thirteen when I met her, at a small parochial high school in the Black Country. She was an expert at mince pies and such things. I remember missing the first play she starred in, something called "The Briary Bush," if I recall correctly. Life is full of missed things and, I suppose, not even theater can show all the things we know nothing about.

5. "Do you ever have the feeling that you are marking time? Perhaps you do. I don't usually, but have had for the past month. I do not find it too comfortable a feeling. I have a Puritan attitude towards waste and a waste of time — we only pass this way once and all that. A lifetime — it must be for something. Now, why did I get on this?"

Marking time while searching for a something, a meaning. This is probably why we have time, to wonder why we have it.

6. We know our friends "by the things they leave behind. I'd like to know more about all the directions you are going in." And I thought that I was going only in one direction. Others often see us better than we see ourselves.

7. I like what Saul Bellow wrote:

Our French friends invariably see the answers to such questions, and all questions of truth, to be overwhelmingly formidable, incongenial, hostile to us. It may be, however, that truth is not always so punitive. . . . There may be truths that are on the side of life. I am quite prepared to admit that, being habitual liars

117

and deluders, we have good cause to fear the truth,
but I am not at all ready to stop hoping. There may be
some truths which are, after all, our friends in the
universe.

What is striking about such a passage is not merely its
warmth, but the fact that we cannot have ideas as friends.
Only persons are friends. The great problem is whether
truth is a person.

8. The Stoics sought to overcome the world by a self-
sufficiency that argued to the reasonableness of all creation:
there is one reason, one law, one brotherhood. What happens
is thus reasonable. We show our mastery in this view by not
allowing ourselves to be affected by passions or emotions.
But then, there are many things we do not want to master.
"Find a little bad in the best of things," someone once wrote
in *Punch*. We are not masters of everything. We are suspi-
cious that something more than reason as we know it rules
the world.

9. "Your trip across America sounds like a *childhood
rediscovered* type. I suppose with enough surviving relatives, the return 'home' is not too melancholic. Somehow
your trip brings to mind a Willa Cather book I read a long
time ago about life on the prairie. — It is interesting how I
have almost a horror of that sort of life, which you seem to
find almost enviable. I suppose it's the people, whom I do not
know. And indeed, that book had a tremendous influence
over my opinions of the area. Also, for a woman, or at least
to me, the life sounds like sheer drudgery, as the book, in
fact, made it out — drudgery and boredom, from which there
was no escape. Simpler people I can really only fully appreciate through your eyes. It is one of your effects on me, to
make me more charitable, more sympathetic toward people,
as you love them so."

I later read some of Hamlin Garland's *Main-Travelled*

Roads, of Iowa and Wisconsin in the early part of this century. My grandparents, uncles, and aunts, my father and mother must have known this life too. I am sure a midwestern life could be all a Willa Cather or Garland described it to be, the kind my friend feared.

Nevertheless, I have loved these relatives of mine and through them their lives. This makes me wonder, at times, if this is not possible in all places, all times. I suspect Scripture means this when it has the Christ to be born in Bethlehem and growing up in Nazareth, places of no account, of drudgery and boredom. Funny, the wife of one of my colleagues was born in Nazareth, the most nonboring person imaginable.

10. One Holy Week, I spent in Naples, a city full of loud voices, ugly buildings, sun, smells of fresh vegetables. The Bay from the hills was as beautiful as the songs about it. Vesuvius was dominant in the distance, but the weather did not allow it to dominate too much. There was a vitality to this city, a sense of lost glory, people hawking things, dirt, grandeur. All was mixed together.

Practically every church had grass or moss growing on its roof-tops and cupolas. They will not be disturbed in their growth. There I heard plaints and dirges that were definitely Arabic, or so I thought. The smell of fresh pizza was everywhere. The spirit is near to the earth in Naples, rooted and holy. There was also much crime in Naples in comparison with the rest of Italy, mostly contraband. Men were always trying to sell me a watch or radio or some other booty.

11. "Dear Uncle Jim,
How are you, I am fine. Would you please
EXCUSE this letter? This is my first time
on a typ writer. Wehave not been down
to the beach since you left.Please
come back soon I sure miss you.
Whats up? any thing new
happen? If so write to me and

119

tell me. Have yyou gone on
anyy vacations latelyor any
        place exciting?
                If anyy thing exciting happens
                you willl be the first to know.

        I have to be going now.
                Good By,
                                Love,
                                        GAil."

Minus one or two dozen erasure marks, this is a first type-
written letter. Gail is out of college now. "If anything exciting happens, you will be the first to know." And what if the
world were such that nothing exciting ever happened—who
would know? Would Uncle Jim?

12. Except for a few years in the Maryknolls, my Aunt
Esther lived in the Midwest. She never was well and had to
leave the convent for health reasons, a kind of infection she
contracted ironically on her journey to the Novitate in New
York. After she died, my Aunt Fran sent me these lines from
Aunt Esther:

"Why does one have to suffer? Why one so much
more than another? All week I have been so very
miserable. Yet, what is really wrong with me? I know
God isn't cruel. He has been exceptionally lenient
with me, and I am very grateful to Him. I am not
complaining now, only wondering the why of it all? I
am grateful for the long days and nights that He
passed by, for time didn't seem to exist. I was hardly
conscious that I was living so that years went by as a
dream. I wasn't conscious of pain or weariness, only of
His great love and understanding. I had everything
that I wanted. I needed nothing, like a child. Maybe
my life was not meant to be exactly like others. I am
ill for a purpose, and I must use it to the best of my

ability. I am still a small child. I love God and He loves me. Nothing more is wanted. Nothing more is needed."

This aunt was part of my childhood. And I saw her fairly often in my travels back and forth across the world before she died. There was always something mysterious about her. And I have seldom seen the Christian meaning of pain better put, undoubtedly because she did know what it meant, while most of the rest of us only speculate about it.

13. Roger Schutz, the Abbot of Taize in France, in a book I slowly was reading in Naples, said:

> Each new day, greet each day anew. Tomorrow will be perhaps the last day of our days among men. It is impossible to live in the today without being aware that it might be our last.
> If we regard tomorrow for that which concerns it, immediately we are invaded by inquietude, incapable of living for the day given, shared only among the contrary pulls toward the past and the future.

Enjoying the day given seems the special virtue of the Neapolitans. While there, one morning about eleven, I was in the Gesu Nuovo. A wedding was in progress. Weddings, I think, change the world, and keep it too. Things happen on particular days. We want, we need to live them, to remember them too.

14. On Holy Thursday in the Church of San Dominico Maggiore, the Church with a crucifix which was said to have talked to St. Thomas, the Mass was sung by a group of girls about ten or so, all dressed in white. The nun who directed them had perfect discipline. This service commemorating the Lord's Last Supper is always moving, with its procession to the Altar of Repose, wherein the Sacrament will be placed until the morrow, the *Pange Lingua*, the candles. Even though the Italians will talk during most any religious serv-

ice, still there was a hush. A girl would see her old aunt or friend's mother. She would come over and chat for a bit. You saw that the old woman was pleased. Those churches in Naples were so large, so familiar that it seemed the normal thing to do, chat a bit.

Sometimes, you could see faces in Italy so calm, so serene that the whole world seemed at peace. Then you could realize that some of the greatest madonnas seen in Italian painting were merely reflections of what was seen in the faces of ordinary women in the streets and churches.

15. Hans Urs von Balthasar said: "But all true fecundity of a life leaps from the decision taken once and for all." At first sight, it seems strange to unite decision and fecundity. Fecundity seems almost to happen out of the effervescence of things, while decision seems almost opposed to fecundity. But fecundity needs to know who we are, who we shall be, where we shall be. We have too little concern often for what we know or hope will come to be. Perhaps that is why some of the translations of *Exodus* describe Yahweh as "I Am Who Will Be." Decision suggests that we are always responsible for more than this world.

16. The noises and smells, both the horrid ones and the delightful ones, of Naples, make it a familiar place. Old men chatting in a bar, while the huge tower bells of Santa Chiara across the street rang out at seven. There were shrill feminine voices, smells of the gaffre doughnuts in the morning with the coffee, the uncollected garbage stench in the rain, garbage in the midst of the local street markets, smells of onions, artichokes, tomatoes, lettuce, finochio, children shouting, running, cries of little boys playing soccer or basketball, the strong cheese smells, the motorcycles that abominate the air, the Neapolitan songs you catch snatches of while ladies hang out their wash, horns always honking, the deep blast of the ships in the distant harbor. The pizzas, in every fourth shop almost, have a smell that kept you hungry all day.

All of these things blended together in a city that has

somehow survived the ages almost better than any other. We are earthy people, and we are meant to be.

17. Italian churches. - Naples has at least five churches of great beauty, San Gregorio Armeno, San Lorenzo, the Gesu, Santa Maria la Nuova, and the Carmine, perhaps also San Dominico Maggiore, plus a host of churches that are small, lovely, quiet — these are often places you can go and just sit. This is not something the Italians themselves do much of, though they do more than their popular image might suggest. But then, these places are made for thousands of things, not just for sitting.

18. I like the reflection of the English writer Richard Rolle, which I came across in Naples:

> In what state may men most love God? I answer: in whatever state it be that men are in the greatest rest of body and soul and least occupied with the needs of business of this world. For the thought of the love of Jesus Christ and of the joy that last forever, seeks rest without that it be not hindered by comers and goers and occupation with worldly things. And it seeks within great silence from noise of covetings and vanities and of earthly thoughts. And all those especially that live contemplative lives seek rest in body and soul. For a great doctor says that they are God's throne who dwell in one state and are not running about, but are established in the sweetness of God's love.
>
> And I have loved to sit, not for penance, nor for fancy that I wished for men to speak of me, nor for any such thing: but only because I loved God more; the comfort of love lasted longer with me than when going or standing or kneeling. For sitting I am most at rest and my heart is most upward.

As I mentioned, I heard somewhere that Naples is the oldest city in the world in a way, the one lived in, never really destroyed, going on and on, never losing completely what went before. Sitting on Holy Thursday Morning in the

Duomo, at the Service of the Chrism, with the huge jugs of holy oils, listening to the long-speaking Archbishop, being aware of the innumerable statues of the saint-bishops of Naples in their niches above, bishops who did the same service in their days, such things only make you able to sit and wonder.

19. Sometimes, it is quite easy to recall our vanities and mistakes. I was reading Benjamin Franklin again. He was constantly talking about the "erratum" he had made, or the series of errata. In retrospect, our own errata are funny enough, but we seldom are in a position to laugh at them. But others can and do. Perhaps it is best this way.

20. After it had been raining for three straight days, evidently in contradition to my San Francisco self, I said to an elderly priest, just to pass the time of day, "The weather is lousy." He replied, " 'When the sun doesn't shine, Naples is not Naples' — this is the saying."

21. Several months previously, I had attended in Oxford the lovely Evensong Service in Christ Church, a Sunday evening. Now that we Roman Catholics have given up such monastic traditions mostly, there is really nothing to take their place of an evening in all of Italy or any place else. The Tenebrae, so haunting in Holy Week, is also gone. Who saves traditions, I wonder?

22. Naples has a tasty sugar doughnut called the gaffre, whose smell I mentioned earlier. It makes the spirit glad that we have bodies. It is so warm and fragrant and delicious of a morning.

23. We choose what we shall be. But there is grace too.

24. The last Sunday in April we had a terrific storm all morning, lightning, thunder that pealed over Rome for seconds. You could barely see the outline of St. Peter's from our roof-top through the rain. The figure of St. Paul himself stood over the city from its perch on the Column of Marcus Aurelius, over off the Corso. On this Column, there is carved a scene of Jove commanding the rain to restore the Roman

soldiers, an incident also attributed to the prayers of the Christian soldiers. I do not know this incident, theological struggles to interpret the rain. Rome is wonderful in a storm. St. Peter's seems reassuring through heavy mist. The Rock in the Storm of the World.

25. What can believers expect of the world? Will it ever really be better or fit as a home to live in? Marcus Aurelius seems weary. Yet, he fights wars, he tries. Rostovzeff ended his book on *Rome* this way:

> Any creative power that remained turned away from this world and its demands and studied how to know God and be united with him. Thus here again, in the case of the Roman Empire, a steady decline of civilization is not to be traced to physical degeneration, or to any debasement of blood in the higher races due to slavery, or to political and economic conditions, but rather to a changed attitude in the minds of men.

I do not believe we need to live in such an either/or world. The service of the world is not enough, but it is worthy and a love of its own.

26. The Patroness of Italy is Catherine of Siena, a doctor of the Church, a mystic, a lady who told off popes, and therefore is an example to us all. Her Feast Day is April 29. She is buried over in Santa Maria sopra Minerva, the lovely Gothic church. Somehow, my siesta lasted too long. It was raining. I walked over to Santa Maria sopra Minerva. This feast was in my day a large civic-ecclesiastical ceremony, an evening Mass with a pagentry. That year, the Mayor of Siena had sent his greetings, the Mayor of Rome was there, as was the General of the Dominicans.

There were quite a few people wandering in and out, Italian-style. The dark blue of the ceiling, an altar full of flowers, enclosed the lovely, seldom heard Gregorian chant of the Mass. The Cardinal Celebrant was the titular head of the

XI

Church, the Vatican Librarian, a Spaniard, Zamora. In his very long sermon, he said that Catherine combined two things — force and tenderness.

I thought about this combination for the rest of the day. The two are not as opposed as I was inclined to think. Then, at the Consecration, a band of medieval herald-dressed trumpeteers blew a lovely, haunting salute on their long, golden horns. This is still a place for majesty, I thought. We would all be weary were there not places and times like this to remind us that this is not our home.

If there were only force, or only tenderness, it would be simple to understand the world about us. But there are both.

27. "Does one's integrity ever lie in what he is not able to do?" Flannery O'Connor asked. "I think that usually it does, for free will does not mean one will, but many wills conflicting in one man. Freedom cannot be conceived simply. It is a mystery and one which a novel, even a comic novel, can only be asked to deepen."

To reflect that sometimes each of us possesses many lives he did not choose to live is right, and more especially to realize that he might well have been happy in many of the alternatives not chosen in fact. The alternative to reality is not always destruction, just as the alternative to one happiness is not always misery. Often, it is also another happiness.

28. "Sure enough. Goodness is for its own sake. To be sought for itself. The seeking of good is confused for humans now. And I think there are some humans who seek evil. This is a *true* mystery for me. Confusion, I can understand, but rejection baffles me."

The good can be rejected. True enough, as the great philosophers maintain, it seems always to be rejected under some guise, some deliberate turning away. But my friend was probably right, both that rejection of the good is baffling, and that some people do choose evil.

29. How is it possible that people love us when we are

not better than we know we can or should be? And yet, even if we have no faults, it does not follow that everyone or anyone would love us, not even quite good people. We always want to take the choice out of something that, in the end, is only choice. "I do not know why I enjoy to hear from you. It was as if I knew you many years before I met you." Some people want to explain this by re-incarnation, which seems logical enough, but rather uninteresting, as it takes the romance out of the one life that we do have.

Nonetheless, I often think that we meet the people we are meant to meet. This means, logically, I suppose, that I was not born to meet Alexander the Great, or the Apostle Philip, or Napoleon III, or my paternal grandfather, or Marcus Aurelius. But the doctrine has two sides. Not everyone loves and admires us, and we are meant to meet those also. We cannot avoid choosing, though we often try. Some do choose evil, as my friend wrote. But the Roman Emperor was right. We do many things wrong, and we should consider this fact once in a while.

XII

How ridiculous and how strange to be surprised at anything which happens in life.
  – Marcus Aurelius, Meditations, XII, 28.

1. To be surprised by anything that happens in life, this is the beginning of wisdom.

2. We should know what to expect. We should know what is in the hearts of men. But even when we know such things, what does happen is not really as we should have predicted. The familiar world is also full of strangeness, ways that are not our ways.

3. Christians are those who believe that everlastingness is full of joy. And it is they who believe that the ultimate joy is a surprise. Against the certitude that we all can understand all there is to know, there is no defense, except the hint that joy is also active in the world, active and we do not know it.

4. At the end of *I Chronicles*, David arranged for the building of the Temple and for handing over his reign to Solomon. He prayed:

> For who am I and who are my people to have the means to give so generously? All comes from you; from your own hand we have given them to you. For we all are strangers before you, settlers only, as all our ancestors were. Our days on earth pass like a

shadow, and there is no hope. Yahweh, our God, this store we have provided to build a house for your holy name, all comes from your hand, all is yours.

This sense that we know little of our origins and our destiny, that we are settlers and strangers, that our days pass like a shadow is very real. All living possesses this experience. Yet, this King had both gratitude and confidence in the midst of a poignant sense of finitude. The astonishing thing is that nothing is cancelled out. We are strangers indeed, and we are given hope.

5. It stormed for the last two days of April, almost a whole week of rain. We know why it rains, I suppose. We are even trying how to control rain so that it falls at night or only where we want it to fall. I, of course, like it to rain often and also in the daytime. Mainly, I like it to rain unexpectedly. I like the sunshine the same way, unexpectedly. I think I prefer the world as it is in this regard. When rains come, we really do not expect them; and when we really cannot do much about them, then our best course is simply to get wet and enjoy them.

6. Creativity means that the structure of things as we know them is not all comprehensive. Tradition means that we should preserve what others have created, while not denying that we too create, not from nothing, but from something.

7. The way the world appears to us is much more the result of the choices we make, the graces we receive, the kind of persons we might be, than anything that the world outside of us itself contains. Or perhaps, it is wiser to suggest, that we are unable to share so much that is given because we do not choose to receive it. In this sense, we really are unequal. I believe that we do not know what we lack. Perhaps this too is a grace. Yet, it is also a suffering.

8. The classical guitar is a most meditative instrument. Emry Rivas played Sor, Albenez, Bach, Cimerossa, Villa

Lobos, Ponce—a couple of others, which I now forget. There were five encores, too many for propriety, I suppose, but I am glad of them. Some things we really do not want to end; to some things, the only proper response is again, again.

Josef Pieper wrote:

> It is the deliberate uselessness of all this that is important, the element of superabundance and exuberance, of noncalculation and even of waste. The first portion of wine is not used, it is not drunk, it is squandered, it is shed onto the sea or the floor as a libation in honor of the gods. In the same way, Christendom did not build practical meeting rooms, but cathedrals. The peal of Notre Dame de Paris has never served as a time-signal; it has always been and still is the expression of worldly jubilation; it is abundance and waste.

A guitar concert too is like this. There is nothing useful about it, a way to "waste our time" it is. What an odd expression! The word, waste, has become almost a dirty word today. Yet, the concept of waste may well be one of the most powerful and profound ones we have. Practically all the things we do that are worthwhile are wastes of time. But then we so easily forget that this is what time is given to us for, to see what we do with it. Think how severely we should be judged if we never did a thing that was not simply useless! We would literally go through life doing nothing for its own sake.

9. We will not be satisfied by anything in the universe such that some time in our actual mortal lives we will have and realize everything. If there is an ultimate response to us, it will come as a surprise, as something we do not expect, control, or even imagine.

10. How many things do we discover because of the enthusiasm and interest of someone else!

11. On the first Sunday of May, I began to read Gregorovius' *Roman Diaries*. When he arrived in Rome, on the

first Sunday there (October 4, 1852), he said: "On Sunday, I strolled here and there to surprise myself by discovering that I was there before, unexpectedly, this or that building which I had only known previously in prints, such as the Column of Trajan, the Pantheon, the Temple of Vesta, the Pyramid of Gaius Cestus." I like this, to surprise one's-self. I had been in Rome for some ten years before I read these famous diaries.

So I thought I should again take a look at what was about the city. The evening before, I heard a lovely concert of madrigal singers in the Hall of the Cancelleria. The next morning, I finally saw Boromini's lofty Chapel of St. Ivo alla Sapienza. From there, I went through the Piazza Navona to Luigi Francese, because the French were holding an important election that day. There in the French church was the glorious Caravaggio, "The Call, Inspiration, and Death of Saint Matthew," all of these were new to me. I was again surprised about how little I knew of this ancient, familiar city.

12. I had been reading Augustine. "When it is considered how short is the span of human life, does it really matter to a man whose days are numbered, what government he must obey, so long as he is not compelled to act against God or his conscience?" In Luigi Francese, there were buried the French soldiers who fell defending the Papal States in the last century. In retrospect, Augustine seems right. It does not matter so much from the perspective of a hundred years or eternity. Yet, there are some not-so-bad governments I still should prefer to avoid, and too few governments, especially modern ones, do not require us to act against God or conscience.

The huge front doors of the Pantheon were open as I walked by. The name of Marcus Agrippa was still across the portal, two thousand years later, even though Agrippa did not build the Pantheon, the place of all the gods. Hadrian was a modest man in some things. Did it matter what even happened in the reigns of Agrippa or Hadrian, or the one of Augustus, or Tiberius, or Marcus Aurelius?

13. "Competition," I said, "I think there is a conspiracy to get rid of competition. It is said to make us nervous; it makes us unequal, corrupts our relationship with others."

"Competition can be very agonizing," my lovely cousin, Mickey, an excellent athlete herself, then visiting Rome, admitted, "but it enables you to place hardship in the right perspective. It enables you to see that things which you think cannot be done, you can do. Without competition, very many excellent things would simply be impossible."

14. A Nigerian student was in my room for a conference. He wrote a decent term paper, but it lacked really good academic form. Too, he tended to unnecessary rhetoric in the worst sense of preaching the cause of his people under the guise of scholarship. He said to me: "I appreciate very much your remarks and thank you for them. I see the importance of them." I was struck by that response. This was a real gentleman.

15. Testimony is basic. And it must be free. I believe the world is a curious place left free so that men really can discover the true and beautiful in things and events about them. This is why it is so important that our testimony be not programmed or censored. The really great sin of the Christian Church structure has been that it makes you wonder, at times, if what you read by any given Christian is his discovery or is his discovery only after approval. We do have a right to know whether a Christian is actually a Christian. This certainly has become a cloudy issue in many ways with the rapid infiltration of ideology into many areas of religious life. But we also have a need to know whether a Christian is free. The one, the testimony, cannot exist without the other, the freedom.

16. I came across this passage in P. G. Wodehouse: "It is a curious law of nature that the most undeserving of brothers always have the best of sisters. Thrifty, plodding

young men, who get up early, and do it now, and catch the employer's eye, and save half their salaries, have sisters who never speak civilly to them except when they want to borrow money. . . ."

I put this on a postcard and sent it to my sister when she lived in Santa Barbara. She would be quite amused about what category her brother, and therefore herself, fell into, as her brother is not thrifty, nor plodding, nor one who gets up particularly early. But sisters are rather one of the best institutions in the human race. The two-child family ideal, of course, eliminates brothers to brothers and sisters to sisters, or sometimes denies brother to sister or sister to brother. This is sad, indeed, one of the saddest things I know, though we must say, if we have brothers or sisters or do not, this too is a gift. These are not choices which depend on us, though the choices of others may depend on us.

17. To get up early in the morning and watch the sun rise (or the earth turn, both miracles of a sort) is an ancient pagan custom all believers should practice once in a while.

18. Don told me that so many students are annoyed because they realize that they miss something, miss something of which they are deliberately deprived by our schools, universities, and our culture. And what they are deprived of is a realization of what men have known and believed, of what they ought to have learned and did not.

19. In the beginning of Solzhenitsyn's *August 1914*, the young idealist youth slips into Tolstoy's park and unexpectedly runs into the old man taking his walk.

"Lev Nikolaevich, I know I'm disturbing your thoughts and your walk — please forgive me. But I've come such a long way and all I want to hear is a few words from your mouth. Tell me if I understand you rightly. What is the aim of man's life on earth?"

That struck me as a powerful scene in a way, not unrelated to the sadness of which I was just speaking. I am not, indeed, so very impressed with the answer Tolstoy gave —

"To serve the good and build the Kingdom of God on earth."
This seems rather hopeless to me. But I am, nonetheless,
struck by the fact that the question was asked at all.

My own answer? That we should be quiet with one another and hope that the little good we know and the kingdom we succeed in building on this green earth are not all
there is. And yet, I am glad for the swifts that flocked about
the Church of the Twelve Apostles which I used to see across
the piazza, out my window in the springtime, against the
rich Roman sky, or for watching the Mississippi flow by the
Clarksville Dam, when the barge broke loose. Somehow, it is
wrong to be entirely discontented when there is so much.

20. The African student said to me earnestly: "Professor
Banfield said in his book that he did not think that most
people from developing countries would ever be able to hope
to achieve the level of development found in the West. I am
very disturbed by this."

I said: "Well, Professor Banfield is a good scholar, and
he has a right to express his judgments. If you disagree with
him, you must understand his evidence and arguments, bas-
ing your position on facts and truths."

The young man accepted this, which impressed me
about him. This is also why, if you tell people that the Kingdom of God is coming on earth, rather soon, you will exclude
most of the human race from what man is about. I would not
want to do this. That is why I have a faith and a philosophy,
not an ideology.

21. Obscurity is often a curse, but sometimes it can be
rather desirable. Marcus Aurelius always seemed to have
borne his rule with reluctance, with the realization that the
public affairs he had to indulge in were what kept him from
real contentment and wisdom. But obscurity is something
else. We should bear the burdens of our kind if we must. Yet,
fame is itself always seen as something of a temptation and
a distraction, a burden. Obscurity is a kind of freedom too.

22. Today, it is popular to argue that God is most pre-

sent where the change and the passions of a time are least present. Nazareth was such a place, such a *no*-place. When we seek to live in London or Rome or San Francisco or Washington or Delhi, we should be aware that somehow in the generations that follow us, they will realize that the heart of man was not in any of these famous places. Nonetheless, famous places cannot be excluded from providence. Christ went to Jerusalem. Paul and Peter went to Rome. Marcus Aurelius ruled from there. The spirit breathes where it will.

23. "Regarding the Chesterton, Lady Garnet, Andrew Howe quotes in your letter, I think that marriage grounds the floating man and frees the grounded woman. He is given safety from total abstraction and she is given security so that she can move out of herself. It is a good bargain, to say the least."

24. I like bells, especially ones that ring in the distance. Bells, particularly church bells, have been mostly silenced, for pragmatic reasons, as we all have watches, or for cultural reasons, as we all want to sleep unmolested on Sunday or any other morning, even though motorcycles can go full blast through our cities at 3 A.M. But in Rome, in the early spring evening, before Pentecost, the bells called us to something else. The whole culture historically agreed that there was something else to be called to, to prayer, to reflection. Sound itself can be beautiful. That is why we make bells, I suppose. Even silence, in a way, needs bells so that we can hear it.

25. The mighty can fall. It is an awesome scene, for men need political power. That such power be equitable and just yet real is the great issue of politics at all time.

In the *Analects* of Confucius, we can read:

> Tzu-kung asked about government. The Master said, sufficient food, sufficient weapons, and the confidence of the common people. Tzu-kung said, Suppose you had no choice but to dispense with one of these three, which would you forgo? The Master said,

Weapons. Tzu-kung said, Suppose you were forced to dispense with one of the two that were left, which would you forgo? the Master said, Food. For from of old death has been the lot of all men; but a people that no longer trusts its rulers is lost indeed. . . .

And Paul said that we should obey the Emperor. I wonder if he meant that there is something worse than bad rulers?

26. Privacy is a crucial need of the person, though in the hands of the courts, it has become a lethal weapon against the unborn of our kind. There are simply things that are no one else's business, and they should not be. But whether we protect or eliminate human life within us, this is more than just our private business. What is private to us is public to the unborn.

Friendship cannot be based on a kind of mathematical *quid pro quo*. We should, of course, trust one another, converse with one another. We are not necessarily alone, at least not always. Yet, we need privacy. No one can demand always our privacy of us, to participate in it, even though there are times when we must be asked to go out of ourselves. When someone does intrude on our privacy, there is no longer any possibility of friendship, which is ever based on nonobligation, on freedom. But it is based on truth too, which is what we have to give and receive in the first place. Truth is that which, when we give it or receive it, takes nothing away, but only adds. Even when we give it away, we keep it.

27. We were in Santa Maria Maggiore. It was late spring, just before my return to the States. It was raining outside. It was good to have someone seeing this most lovely basilica for the first time when I was perhaps seeing it for the last. Things become ours, in a way, when we have been there, our own history, our own planning and bad planning.

28. "Sometimes, it seems like I'm tired in every way there is. I'm young and yet so tired. Isn't that awful? Dis-

maying is what it is. How did you get to where you are and not be tired? Sometimes the thought of so much future devastates me. . . ." This is a curious notion, that so much future devastates. I am a Christian. That is, I believe in eternity, not in the future. Future is merely time ahead of us. Eternity is everlastingness, a now, a purpose, a reason why anything exists at all, like sitting in the Piazza Navona, late at night, and just gazing at it, or watching on Baker Beach the sun go down over the Pacific.

29. Once, I saw a play in England called, "Turn On." One of the characters in it said, "Don't you sometimes feel the next person walking down the street leads a more real life than you?" Of course, we often feel this, I do anyhow. But it is not so. Reality is not what distinguishes one life from another. We do the thinking, the doing, and the being. What we do, ultimately, distinguishes us, do and think. Augustine would have agreed, I think.

30. The first thing is that we are free. We choose. On the way from Chicago to Milwaukee, I heard, overheard, the following "theological" discussion.

Carrie (age 7): "I can't help what I think, Paul; God makes me think what I think."

Paul (age 9): "No, no, Carrie, that would mean that God was treating us like puppets and he doesn't do that."

Mary Ellen (undisclosed age): "What do you think he does, Paul?"

Paul: "He gives us ourselves, and we do the thinking and the doing."

31. I also saw Herb Gardner's *Thieves* in New York, which believed that every year we live is, in fact, an "extra year." Each year is one that we should not expect to have had in the first place, one that we should be grateful for, a year so surprising that we could never have imagined it possible by ourselves, before the living, even after the living.

32. How do we appear to others? We know our faults, even if we do not admit them. Indeed, we probably know them well enough to cloud our vision of ourselves. "Why are you not tired of life?" as someone once asked me. I never actually thought I needed a reason not to be.

33. I received these lines almost two decades ago now, I had almost forgotten them:

"Yesterday evening, I saw "The Lover" by Harold Pinter. Partly amusing dialogue but depressing after all. The same is true for the Albee play. The simple conclusion seems to be that you better never get married. Or if you take it in a broad sense, that no human relationship, whatever it is like, can finally help you to avoid feelings of forelornness, boredom, and fear. I still cling a bit to the illusion that this is not so, but I am not sure about it. The most positive character in Albee's drama for me was an alcoholic. She had at least found a technique to live with.

". . . I envy you quite often, your open-mindedness and interest in all variety of things. This may be a technique of life as well (I know it is not for you). At Emmendingen, a psychiatrist told me that she believed that we really are not interested in anything for itself, but only as it is a means for us, as it has got a certain function. I do not believe that this is true for everybody, but probably for many people. Unfortunately, I seem to belong to the majority. . . ."

What I mostly want to say is this — that there are things that we should see for themselves, as Aristotle told us, that we need to be interested in a wide variety of things. I still think this. The variety of these things about us is astonishing, and we should see it, praise it, even late in this century.

And yet, how little we know. And we do see that our friends sometimes become tired. There is no way in our time, or in Marcus Aurelius' time or any other time, to escape our limitedness and our failures. That is one of our dignities, perhaps our main one. We are still Christians. And we are still restless. But the reason we will not ultimately be sad, I think, even though there is a lot of sadness among us, is because we know there is a joy in our weakness. We do not "know" it, on second thought, we have been told this. It is something revealed to us, but for us still to understand.

34. In Iowa, my cousin, Franny, took me through his corn and soybean fields, fields, I suspect, which will prove to be crucial places in the coming years because of their incredible productivity. My cousin showed me how a hail storm had clipped off the young shoots, the way the replanted seed was also sprouting. This was one of the few cousins I have who remained a farmer, though he too is now in town, mostly due to the cost of farming by one's-self. I have always admired my farmer cousins' familiarity with things growing, with what the soil will yield and what you must do to work it.

We then drove the tractor. He had a new John Deere. He let me drive it over to see his herd of shorthorn beef cattle. There was a new calf born the night before, lying in the tall grass. My cousin jumped off the tractor, went over and picked it up in his arms. Then he stood it on its wobbly legs. I still have a photo of it, touching sight, really.

35. Not too far away, I visited the lovely graveyard with stones marking my ancestors — mother, grandparents, uncles, great-grandparents, aunts, cousins. It seemed that everyone in that cemetery in Pocahontas County was related to me, in some way or another. Many of those long dead relatives had too, like my cousin, planted and plowed in this black soil where they now rest in peace. The day I was there was quiet and warm. My Aunt Fran recalled to me who each person was — the family of grandmother's brother, a half-brother to my father's cousin, married to my cousin's daughter in a different line.

With my cousin Vincent and his wife, Wilma, we had

visited the Church on the Lizard, the first church in that part of Northwest Iowa, some twenty miles from this cemetery where my mother and grandparents were buried. Both sets of my grandparents, I believe, had been married in the Church "on the Lizard," an expression I often recall my grandmother using. The "Lizard" turned out to be a small creek. In middle age, in the last years of the twentieth century, it is no small thing to find your four grandparents, your mother, buried but a few yards from each other under well-kept lawns.

Such are the places where we all end, if we are lucky. This, too, is a surprise. We cannot really imagine that this eventually will be so. It is about tombs and graves of our kind and kin that all faith depends. To be a Christian in this time too, still means, I think, that we see here, in such a lovely place, a beginning as well as our end.

36. "You wrote something about things not being missed, saying, 'Do not miss some things—they only go around once, or *twice*.' About this 'going around' stuff, there is a saying in my family (it is not original, I think), but it goes like this: 'You only go around once and if you do it right, once is enough.' I think your go-around-once stuff is not a repeat or a return to other places. Everything happens only once. Each thing that happens is new. What do you think?"

Well, I agree, of course.

37. Some time ago, as I mentioned at the beginning of these reflections, these meditations, when I was on the Capitoline Hill in Rome, I caught a side glimpse of the bronze statue of Marcus Aurelius, a sight which seemed unusual to me at the time. The statue seemed brighter, more golden somehow.

I would have thought nothing further on this, except that I came across an article in *La Stampa* about this golding phenomenon, a strange article in a way. The statue did in fact seem at the time to be becoming more golden through

141

some inexplicable natural process. So it was not just in my imagination. Indeed, there appears to be a long and ancient tradition that, when this particular statue turns to gold again, the world will end. The Venerable Bede had related a similar tradition about the Colosseum, that when it falls, Rome will likewise fall.

Marcus Aurelius is the only bronze equestrian statue that has survived from ancient Rome. This statue was once thought to be that of Constantine the Great, the first Christian Emperor, as I mentioned earlier, which probably kept it from being melted down. It was first set up in Rome in A.D. 161, the first year of Marcus Aurelius' reign. In A.D. 400, it was before the Basilica of John Lateran, where it remained until Michaelangelo persuaded Paul III to allow him to place it in the beautiful square, where we can now see it.

The tradition about this golding statue is a myth, of course. This noble and sad emperor, however, whose wonderful image still overlooks this ancient city in a hauntingly beautiful place I have often visited, whose meditations we have pondered so carefully, does remind us still that it will all end somehow. We are here for a purpose. We do not go on and on. We are given ourselves to do the thinking and the doing. We do not know why we are not tired, when so many of our friends are. Each thing happens only once. Everything that happens is new.

38. Marcus Aurelius brooded that we should not be surprised at anything that happens to us.

In the end, however, I think this is not so. For the most astonishing thing is still that there is anything at all, including ourselves, including our friends, including why we are still lonely when we have been given so much, including what happens to us. We should, finally, retain our capacity to be surprised at all these things that do happen, a capacity we should exercise very often, in what we do with our days and years.

Such are these *Meditations Late in the Twentieth Century*. They are, as I say, like life itself, quite unexpected.